CONTENTS

Pg 28 - Joan Tough

LITERACY
A SYSTEMATIC START

LITERACY
A SYSTEMATIC START

ELIZABETH HUNTER-GRUNDIN

Harper & Row, Publishers

London   New York   Hagerstown   San Francisco

Copyright © 1979 E Hunter-Grundin

All rights reserved
First published 1979
Harper & Row Ltd
28 Tavistock Street
London WC2E 7PN

British Library Cataloguing in Publications Data
Hunter-Grundin, Elizabeth
    Literacy
    1 Reading (Preschool)
    2 Reading (Elementary)
    I Title
    372.4   LB1140.5.R4

ISBN 0-06-318128-2
      0-06-318140-1 Pbk

ISBN

Designed by R Dewing 'Millions'
Typeset by Inforum Ltd, Portsmouth
Printed and bound by The Garden City Press, Letch-
worth

Chapter 9

**"Teaching and learning are
mainly language games
in which the stakes are high –
a true education."**

Smith, Goodman and Meredith
Learning and Thinking in the Elementary School.'

FOREWORD

This book has as its aim the description of the means through which the author believes that early education in language and literacy can be most successful, the presentation of the theories and ideas that underpin this belief, and the empirical evidence accumulated by the author. The empirical evidence is the product of many years of classroom teaching, of teacher education at initial and inservice levels, and of research.

The research project described in Chapter 8 has been given considerable prominence because it is an important and 'recordable' part of the empirical evidence supporting the author's approach. The other parts of the evidence are also important, but since, like most personal experience accumulated over a number of years, it does not lend itself to precise recording in so many words and figures, it does not feature as prominently in the written account.

I wish to convey my very sincere gratitude to several people whose help and support enabled me to complete my research project. Professor Denis Lawton of the University of London Institute of Education supervised the study with energy, interest, and insight. My friends and colleagues Tony Davies, Marjorie Davies, Joyce Hidden, and Jill Whittard helped me to test so many young pupils individually, and to score the results. My mother, Helen Moss, and my friend Eve Guy helped to record data at various stages, and to check and recheck lists of scores.

I owe a very special debt of gratitude to my husband, Dr. Hans U. Grundin, of the Open University Institute of Educational Technology. An experienced and gifted educational researcher, he has provided guidance and constructive criticism throughout the writing of this book.

Peggy Hall and her team of teachers at Bessemer Grange Infant School have been a continuous source of enthusiasm and inspiration. The research project was carried out without funding or working time allocation, and any value that it has in contributing to the evidence in support of a systematic language-based approach to literacy is entirely due to the cooperation and collaboration of all the London teachers who were part of it. To them, and to the children taught by them, I record my very deep gratitude.

Elizabeth Hunter-Grundin

CHAPTER 1
READING: A LANGUAGE GAME

A quick look in any handbook on the teaching of reading reveals that there are many different views regarding what is the best method, and it often seems to be assumed that the choice of method must be left to the personal taste and preference of the individual teacher. Some of the methods of teaching reading are merely different roads meant to lead to the same goal, but there are also differences of opinion regarding what the goal is. And these differences stem mainly from the lack of agreement concerning the nature of reading. It is, therefore, important that anyone who wants to present a case for a certain approach to the teaching of reading should make it clear from the outset what the goal is, what kind of 'reading' is to be taught.

My approach to reading and the teaching of reading is based firmly on the premise that reading is a *language and communication process*. It is one of the four aspects of language usage, the other three being speaking, listening, and writing. Few people would deny that reading is *part of* a language and communication process, but many define it rather narrowly as only the initial stage in that process. In one of the most widely used books on the teaching of reading published in Britain, Moyle (1970) writes:

Writing is the process of presenting speech in a more permanent visual form and therefore *reading* can be looked upon as the reverse of this process, namely, *turning the collection of symbols seen upon a piece of paper into 'talk'*, or, in the case of silent reading, *into an image of speech sounds*.

According to this view, reading is simply a translation process, the outcome of which is spoken language or a 'silent image' of spoken language. The main part of the communication process, i.e., understanding what the written message means, is something which follows after the reading, a thinking process which is separate from the reading process. This view can be schematically illustrated as follows:

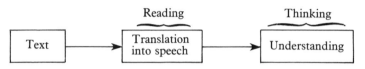

From this view it follows that the teaching of reading should concentrate on the translation phase, on how the units of written language (the letters) relate to those of spoken language (the sounds). This phase is often called 'decoding', because it is supposed to involve going from the unfamiliar, 'secret' code of written language to the familiar code of spoken language. Teaching of reading as 'decoding' usually results in considerable emphasis on the so-called 'mechanics' of reading, which can best be mastered through extensive drill of grapheme-phoneme correspondences and so on.

The view taken here does not deny that an element of 'decoding' is involved in reading. Neither does it deny that translation from written symbols to speech sounds often occurs when the reader tries to make sense of the written words. What it *does* deny is that the translation/decoding phase of reading can be isolated from the comprehension phase. Instead of the previous illustration which shows 'reading' followed by 'thinking', the alternative view can be illustrated like this:

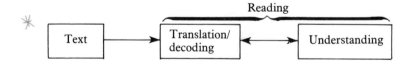

The reading process includes both 'translation/decoding' and 'understanding', and these two phases of reading are interrelated in a rather complex way. 'Decoding' can certainly facilitate understanding, in the sense that the pronunciation of a letter configuration can help us to understand it. But the relationship can also operate the other way round. Understanding what a letter configuration means can help us to translate it correctly into speech sounds. For example, the letter combination 'row' is 'decoded' in one way if it has to do with 'moving a small boat forward', and in another way if has to do with 'conflict or disagreement'.

The main reason for defining 'reading' so that it comprises the entire process involved in understanding written language is, then, that the 'understanding aspect' permeates the entire process, so that it is impossible to say at what stage understanding begins, or at what stage other aspects of the process end.

The narrow definition of reading as 'decoding' is rejected also because it is based on the rather dubious assumption that reading always involves – and should involve – translation of letter combinations into speech sounds. The fluent reader can 'take in' and understand words at a much higher rate than he could possibly pronounce them. And it is perfectly possible to understand words in print without knowing how to pronounce them, or when pronouncing them wrongly.

To reject the narrow view of reading as 'decoding' has important consequences for the teaching of reading. If reading is a language and communication process where understanding is always interwoven with other aspects of the process, it follows that the teacher of reading must not try to separate the 'decoding' aspects of reading from the 'understanding' aspects. Drill of the mechanics of reading is seen to be of highly dubious value, even positively harmful, if it leads to neglect of the most important outcome of reading: *understanding*.

The view of reading taken here is often described as '*psycholinguistic*'. This description derives from the disciplines psychology and linguistics. From psychology there is the theory that most children have a predilection for 'making meaning', and that this helps to motivate a problem-solving approach to understanding written language. From linguistics there is the hypothesis that familiarity with the patterns and rhythms of language functions as a cueing system which helps the reader to predict what an unknown word is likely to be.

For example, when confronted by the sentence,

The frightened boy ran through the park

the pupil would be encouraged to use problem-solving strategies to arrive at the meaning of the words in that sentence which he did not know as part of his sight vocabulary. If the pupil did not know the words 'frightened' and 'through', the teacher using a psycholinguistic approach would ask him to read as much of the sentence as he could. The pupil would then read

The . . . . boy ran . . . . the park.

Taking the second of the two unknown words first, the teacher would ask the pupil what the word could *possibly* be, and solutions like

in the park or
up the park

might be suggested. The actual word is much longer than either of the two suggested, and knowing the 'kind' of word it must be (without necessarily being able to describe it as a 'preposition'), it is likely that the pupil is able to predict the word 'through'. Some knowledge of phonic word attack skills would be helpful in providing the information that the word begins with the sound 'th-' as in 'three'.

As for the first of the two unknown words, *'frightened'*, the pupil would know from his familiarity with the structure of language that this word will tell us something about the boy. It is likely that at least one cue to this word will be found in the passage preceding this sentence, so that the teacher is able to ask the pupil.

How do you think the boy is feeling?

Once again the phonic word attack skill to recognize the initial f-sound (or the consonant cluster 'fr-') would provide another useful cue to the missing word.

It should be noted that teaching in this way helps the pupil to develop independent problem-solving strategies when he is reading silently, without the help of another person. The pupil learns techniques for deriving meaning by means of the cues available to him, including picture cues (illustrations) where these exist. This helps the pupil to become a more confident reader. Especially in the early stages, he should be given praise for an *intelligent* guess, which provides the correct meaning, even if his 'reading' of the word is inaccurate. With more practice, and with more skill in phonic analysis, he will achieve word-for-word *accuracy*, as well as correct meaning. For example, a pupil might read the sentence discussed earlier

The *scared* boy ran through the park.

He should be encouraged and praised for finding the correct meaning of the sentence. Depending upon how much progress he is making, the teacher may say

> Good! That's what the word *means*. That's fine. But have another look at it. What is the *first sound*, do you think? (Pupil answers). Now, is there a word which means 'scared' and which begins with the sound 'f-'?

The psycholinguistic view of reading is consistently and comprehensively developed in a number of books by Frank Smith (1971, 1973, and 1978). A psycholinguistic view of reading is also the basis for the important contributions in the field of teaching of reading made by Kenneth and Yetta Goodman, who are perhaps best known for the 'miscue analysis' research work.

In an attempt to synthesize what they regard as the best features in a number of theoretical models of reading, Dechant and Smith (1977) rely heavily on the psycholinguistic approach as having the 'most to offer in reading instruction'. They describe the approach briefly as follows:

> It suggests that reading involves a basic knowledge of language as well as the utilization of complex active perceptual and cognitive strategies of information selection and processing. Reading is an active cognitive skill.

Using a somewhat provocative, and perhaps too easily misunderstood, phrase, the Goodmans have called reading 'a psycholinguistic guessing game'.

In this 'game' the player, i.e., the reader, has to use all available strategies in order to derive meaning from the printed text. Some of these strategies involve predicting or formulating hypotheses, and testing the predictions or hypotheses. That is where the 'guessing' comes into the game. It is not a question of 'wild' guessing. It is rather a question of utilizing all available knowledge, and then, when some uncertainty still remains, making an intelligent guess about the meaning of a word or phrase. But the 'game' does not stop at the guessing stage; it also involves confirmation of the 'guesses' in the light of later parts of the text.

In order to avoid the notion that this approach to reading encourages errors and discourages accuracy, it might be better to describe reading as 'a psycholinguistic *guessing-and-checking* game'.

This would emphasize that reading involves making guesses about meaning as we go along, but also continuously trying to check, and if necessary revise, these guesses as more and more cues to the meaning are picked up from the text. It is important to note in this context that this 'guessing-and-checking' is not unique to reading. It also characterizes listening. When we hear spoken language, we cannot always expect to pick up the complete message without any errors or omissions. We must therefore be prepared to restore or re-create the spoken message on the basis of all sorts of cues, and this involves making guesses about what exactly has been said.

We may believe that we understand spoken language on the basis of a complete, error-free 'reception' of the speech sounds. But as soon as we have to receive a spoken message with a minimum of context, we realize how difficult it is to hear what people say. The most common example is probably our difficulty in catching the name of a person being introduced to us. If we have no prior knowledge or expectation about the person's name, the introduction amounts to having to identify a sound combination that is picked at random from among several thousand possible sound combinations. The result is, as we all know, that often we do not catch a person's name when we hear it for the first time.

Reading and listening are, then, *language games* of the same basic type, although they differ in terms of the cues to meaning that are available to the 'player', i.e., the reader or the listener. The purpose of the game can in either case be said to be *reduction of uncertainty* about meaning. All approaches to reading probably accept that reduction of uncertainty is the goal of reading, but some approaches tend to see it as an all-or-none situation; that is, either there is complete certainty (the reader/listener *knows* what the message is) or there is complete uncertainty (the reader/listener *does not know* what the message is). The psycholinguistic approach, on the other hand, presupposes that uncertainty can be *gradually reduced*, and that some reduction of uncertainty can be worthwhile, even if it does not result at once in complete certainty. Naturally, the player of this kind of language game aims at deriving as much as possible of the meaning conveyed by the speaker/writer. But the beginning player should not be labelled as a failure simply because he does not immediately derive the full, correct meaning. As long as he has derived *a* meaning, he has made some progress, and guided by the teacher he should be able to develop more and more his ability to play the game and become a successful reader.

This view of reading as a language game implies that the player/reader can use *all available cues to meaning* as he goes along. And this is true of the beginning reader as well as the fluent adult reader. In those approaches to the teaching of reading which emphasize the 'decoding' of letter into sound, the reader is not encouraged to use all sorts of cues. One the contrary, he is taught to concentrate solely on the *graphophonic* cues within each single word. This concentration on only one type of cue to meaning makes the game a much more difficult one, particularly for the very young children who are not very good at the kind of analysis needed to capitalize on the graphophonic cues.

With a psycholinguistic approach, reading becomes a language game where the reader, from the very beginning, is encouraged actively to use cues from each of the three main cueing systems:

1   The semantic cueing system

This system is very closely linked to the syntactic cueing system, so closely that it might even be argued that they should be regarded as aspects of one large 'syntactic-semantic' cueing system. The semantic cueing is based on the reader's knowledge of the vocabulary or the 'lexicon' of his language. Like the knowledge about syntax, the knowledge about lexicon is normally implicit. Most people would find it extremely difficult to give an explicit definition of the word 'chair', but they have usually no doubt about what the meaning of the word is. The semantic cueing system does not only presuppose familiarity with the words used in a text. It also presupposes understanding of the *concepts* to which the words relate. It is possible to recognize a word like 'system' without difficulty, but still fail to have any understanding of the concept 'system'. In order to be able to utilize the semantic cues, the reader must, then, have some understanding of the concepts used by the writer as well as some familiarity with the words used to express the concepts.

2   The syntactic cueing system

This enables the reader to utilize his knowledge of 'patterns' of language, of the ways in which words can be linked together to form meaningful utterances. Every user of a language has an implicit knowledge of its 'grammar', and an important part of that grammar is the syntax. Since children become speakers and listeners long before they become readers, their knowledge of grammar is based on the spoken language. The better the command of spoken language, the more easily the beginning reader can use the syntactic cueing system, provided, of course, that the printed language corresponds closely enough in its syntax to the spoken language of the beginning reader.

3 *The graphophonic cueing system*

This makes use of cues within single words in the form of letter-sound relationships. The graphophonic cueing can be more or less complete. It can amount to a full 'decoding' of an unfamiliar word, leading to a correct pronunciation, e.g., of the word 'system'. Or it can simply amount to the reader utilizing the cue entailed in the initial letter, e.g., realizing that 'dog' in the sentence 'On the farm were many animals, cows, pigs, cats, and a dog' is an animal that begins with the sound 'duh'.

To these three main cueing systems should probably be added a fourth system which might be called the *situational cueing system*. This system comprises a wide range of cues to meaning which are not entirely linguistic in nature. The cues derive from our knowledge about the society we live in and its culture (or cultures, if we live in a multicultural society). It relates to our knowledge of all kinds of habits and conventions, including conventions about language style, e.g., knowing that the language of poetry differs considerably from that of textbooks in areas like computer programing and automobile repairing.

All these cueing systems are used concurrently by the mature reader, although he may be totally unaware of using them. The efficient reader typically utilizes the minimum of cues needed to reconstruct the meaning of the printed words. He rarely utilizes all the cues available to him. In particular, the efficient reader tends to rely a great deal on syntactic and semantic cues, and on situational cues, but not very much on graphophonic cues. In other words, the symbols that he can actually see on the paper constitute only a part of the total 'input' that enables the reader to reconstruct the meaning, the message conveyed by the writer. This is what led Frank Smith to formulate his apparently paradoxical statement: 'Reading is only partly visual.'

Implications for teaching

The view taken here that reading is a language game where the player/reader uses a wide range of cues from several different areas in order to reduce as much as possible his initial uncertainty about the meaning of the text has important consequences for the teaching of reading. It strongly suggests that in order to help a pupil or student to become a more proficient reader it is important to adopt teaching strategies by which he will be encouraged and enabled to make maximum use of the syntactic and semantic cueing systems, and minimal use of the graphophonic system. It follows that reading tasks should be presented in the form of meaningful flowing prose which corresponds as far as possible to the pupil's spoken language. Pupils should not be required to 'read' or to attempt to understand words written or printed in isolation, because two of the major cueing systems are thereby denied to them. Also, from the pedagogic point of view, it follows that the more control the learner has of his spoken language, and the greater his background of experiences, the less visual detail he will require in order to gain understanding of the text, and hence the more proficient his reading skill will become. With less dependence upon the detailed visual cueing of the graphophonic system, and more reliance upon the language-based syntactic and semantic cueing systems, reading skill in terms of comprehension should develop and mature according to the needs and dictates of his interests and environment.

Another factor which can facilitate reading for meaning is redundancy – the providing of numerous cues to the same information. This is a feature of both written and spoken language which helps the learner to derive meaning, because the concept is presented in more than one form in order that the reader may respond to at least one description or presentation of it. The efficient reader may use redundancy, when necessary, by postponing or deferring jnudgement concerning meaning, and reading further into the text in order to gain comprehension. Conversely, the efficient reader may skim redundant passages, if this stategy is appropriate for his reading purpose at that time and does not impair his understanding.

This view of reading presupposes a flexible 'information-gathering' approach, employing the most appropriate cueing systems to maximum advantage in each particular reading situation. Emphasis is on meaning rather than on words, and it is claimed that often the best way to discover the meaning of a word is to read the whole sentence in which it appears. And if the meaning of a sentence is not fully clear, the most productive way of trying to understand it more fully is usually to read more of the paragraph in which the sentence is placed – or sometimes even to read the following paragraph.

Flexibility is a key word in more than one respect in this approach to reading. When reading is narrowly defined as 'decoding' from letter to sound, the emphasis is nearly always on a strictly 'linear' progress through the text. The words are read one by one from left to right in the exact order in which they are printed, and the lines are read from the top towards the bottom of the page. If the reader lets his eye wander back to something he has already read, then, according to this view of reading, this is a 'defect in his reading behaviour'. From a psycholinguistic viewpoint the interpretation is rather different. The reader is still expected to start from the beginning of the text and work towards the end, but to go back and reread something is not regarded as 'deficient reading behaviour' but probably as a sensible way of trying to find more cues to the meaning of a sentence or passage.

To see reading as a language game which is 'played for meaning' does not imply taking reading less seriously than if the emphasis is on the mechanics of memorizing grapheme-phoneme correspondences. But it does imply taking the totality of the reading process into account. And it implies recognizing that reading is an interesting, meaningful activity with its focus constantly on *communication*, from one person to another, of something that is worth communicating.

CHAPTER 2
READING READINESS: WHAT ARE WE WAITING FOR?

A state of confusion

In one of the major works on reading readiness published in Britain, Downing and Thackray (1975) define reading readiness as follows:

> the stage in the child's development when, either through maturation or through previous learning, or both, the individual child can learn to read easily and profitably.

Many similar definitions are to be found in the literature on the teaching of reading in general. For example, Moyle (1968) describes the idea of reading readiness as:

> that point in a child's life when his abilities and skills are sufficiently developed, his personality adquately stable and his interests sufficiently lively for him to make a successful start on his first reading book

Definitions of this kind may be treated with a certain measure of oversimplification and interpreted as meaning simply:

> reading readiness is the time when a child is ready to read.

Such a definition is, of course, not very helpful in a practical teaching situation. Alternatively, the examination of definitions of this kind may result in a series of questions which prove difficult, if not impossible, to answer. For example:

1 which abilities and skills are relevant in this context?

2 how do we know when a skill or abiltiy is 'sufficiently' developed?

3 which facets of the child's personality should be included in the assessment?

4 how do we judge if personality traits are 'adequately' stable?

5 is there a 'point' in every child's life when all these conditions operate?

6 if so, how do we *recognize* that point?

Many more questions of this kind could be listed, but those stated above should be sufficient to show that a cloud of ambiguity surrounds the whole issue of reading readiness and its relation to the teaching of reading. Typically, student teachers are instructed to wait for four separate categories of maturity to develop in a child before any 'formal' teaching of reading should begin. Exactly what is meant by 'formal' teaching in this context is rarely, if ever, discussed, nor is the appropriateness of the concept of 'formality' questioned. I was taught, as a student teacher, to remember the four kinds of maturity by the mnemonic device 'PIES', representing

*P*hysical maturity;

*I*ntellectual maturity;

*E*motional maturity;

*S*ocial maturity.

As I took this down carefully in my notebook, I remember being mildly surprised at the fact that so many of us had ever managed to pass muster and been deemed 'ready to read'. The mnemonic 'PIES' may not be used in today's teacher training, but the four areas of maturity involved in reading readiness are still listed by writers in the field, as for example in Carrillo (1978), where the order of the four areas is changed to 'IPES', but the areas are still the same.

Of course, healthy growth within each of the areas is essential for the general education of the child, and during all the stages of that growth the child is *maturing* and *learning*, through a natural interaction with his environment. The adults who are his first 'teachers', usually his parents, enable and facilitate the child's learning by stimulating his interests, responding to these interests, and by creating an environment conducive to communication.

In this way children learn to speak. We do not wait for 'speaking readiness' to occur through some kind of automatic process. Nor do we administer special tests to find out if a child is ready to learn how to speak and how to communicate through the use of language. We speak to them and we communicate with them. If they are interested and excited by the communication through language, they learn how to participate in that communication.

Reading is communication in a very different, and in some ways more difficult code, i.e., the letters and other signs of written language. But the problem facing the child is similar to that facing the child when learning to speak, and the same kind of stimulation is needed. In learning to read, as in learning to speak, an interest must be created in the child, and a desire to participate in this particular form of communication. Undefined or vaguely defined notions of maturity in the physical, intellectual, emotional, or social area can in no way give an indication of the strength of a child's desire to communicate or his need to 'make meaning' of language communication, whether spoken or written. When the motivation is sufficiently strong, the child will respond to the 'stimulus' of written language, and that response denotes the most important aspect of his *readiness to learn*.

Motivation, then, makes the child 'ready to learn', but there must also be *something to respond to*. Motivation and learning cannot occur in a vacuum. When the motivation starts to grow, the child must be surrounded by examples of communication through the written word. He must be able to see that written language is a natural part of everyday life, something people use for various purposes, not as an end in itself but as a means to communication.

Criteria of reading readiness

Goodacre (1967) found that in England the concept of reading readiness is widely accepted by teachers. Her survey indicated that a majority of teachers at the infant level subscribe to the idea of a 'teachable moment', a time when a beginning can most profitably be made to the task of teaching children to read. This 'teachable moment' was commonly believed to occur, for most children, around the age of six years, but teachers generally found it very difficult to explain how this 'moment' can be recognized.

Some of the teachers in Goodacre's survey suggested developmental characteristics which could help in identifying the elusive 'teachable moment'. The most frequently mentioned characteristics were:

1   attitude to reading activities (interest)
2   perceptual abilities I (recognition of words out of context)
3   perceptual abilities II (knowledge of letter sounds and shapes)
4   ability to handle reading materials (e.g., careful handling of books)
5   spoken language development (vocabulary and speech)
6   adjustment ot the school situation
7   general attitude to the school environment
8   intellectual ability
9   interest in writing activities

It is worth emphasizing that not a single one of the schools surveyed by Goodacre used any kind of test of reading readiness. Pupil 'attitude' and 'interest' featured most frequently in the questionnaire replies as indicators of readiness, and teachers relied solely on their own subjective judgement in the assessment of attitude and interest. Like all subjective judgements, teachers' judgements of attitude and interest in the field of reading may sometimes be arbitrary and erratic, but these judgements can also be informed and reliable. It should be remembered that we depend upon the same judgements for decisions concerning many other important aspects of education. The ability to make informed judgements is a crucial part of teacher professionalism. A high degree of professional expertise is particularly important in the context of nursery and infant education, and the reading readiness problem is only one of many manifestations of this need.

The aforementioned nine-point list quoted from Goodacre (1967) merits a closer analysis. The first four points on the list imply some knowledge about reading, or even some reading ability. If these four characteristics are regarded as *prerequisites* for teaching of reading, are teachers not in fact waiting until children acquire some reading ability before the teachers find it worthwhile trying to teach them to read? Perhaps the idea is that children should acquire 'informally' some understanding of reading before 'formal' teaching of reading begins.

It is true that many children acquire some reading skills at home before they are taught any reading skills in school – sometimes even before they begin school. These privileged children may well be ready to develop their reading skills further through 'formal' teaching. But what about all those children who are not in that way priviledged, who do not learn anything about reading in their homes, neither 'formally' nor 'informally'? How are they to develop the understanding of reading which is supposed to be a prerequisite for reading readiness?

It is also important to note that perceptual abilities feature twice in the Goodacre list of characteristics, first in relation to *words out of context*, and then in relation to *letter sounds and shapes*. These criteria of readiness presuppose a certain amount of teaching, at least the kind of informal teaching provided by some parents. This means that the child's own growth or maturation is not enough for him to reach readiness in this respect; active intervention of an adult is usually needed.

The perceptual criteria of reading readiness listed by Goodacre are also directly related to specific methods of reading instruction. The first criterion relates to the 'look-and-say' method, which builds on recognition of isolated words, and the latter criterion relates to the phonics method, which puts great demands on the beginning reader's ability to analyse and synthesize the components of spoken and written language (i.e., sounds and letters).

The phonics method involves:

a)   focusing attention on each word individually, disregarding context cues

b)   analysing the word into single letters and/or appropriate groups of letters

c)   attaching a sound – or a blend of two sounds – to each letter or group of letters

d)   linking or blending the identified sounds into one integrated complex of sounds

e)   recognizing the integrated or synthesized complex of sounds as a meaningful word

For example, on encountering the word

p a r k

the pupil must make the following letter-sound 'correspondences' by means of analysis:

letter 'p' – sound 'puh'

letter 'a' – sound 'ah'

letter 'r' – sound 'ruh'

letter 'k' – sound 'kuh'

The analysis must take into account that only one of the several possible 'sound values' of the letter 'a' is appropriate. If the child lives in a region where the 'r' in 'park' is not pronounced at all (which is true of many parts of England), the 'r' must be recognized as having an influence on the 'a', while being silent itself. The child *cannot* rely on it that 'par' should be pronounced 'p-ah' ('p' followed by a long, open 'ah'), because other words beginning with 'par' do not follow such a rule. Take, for example, the word 'parent'. How to pronounce 'par' depends entirely on what comes after.

There are many more complications involved in the analysis of letter-sound 'correspondences', and after the analysis comes the daunting task of synthesizing the four sound units into one word, 'park', possibly leaving one of the units out (the 'ruh' sound). Without going into further details, it should be obvious that this approach to beginning reading confronts the young pupil with a highly abstract and very complex task. It must be emphasized that this task is not just a *perceptual* task, but a sophisticated *conceptual* or *intellectual* task.

There comes a stage in reading development when the analytic perceptual-conceptual skill involved in phonics becomes valuable, perhaps even indispensable as one of the 'tools' for coping with unfamiliar words. At this stage a phonics approach should be very helpful. But why should we consider this advanced perceptual-conceptual skill as a *prerequisite* for our beginning to teach children how to extract meaning from written words?

Prereading skills

It has been known for a long time that small children are ill equipped for abstract learning. In the Soviet Union Vygotsky (1962) carried out research which attempted to account for the tremendous lag between children's spoken language and their ability to cope with written language:

> Our studies show that it is the abstract quality of written language that is the main stumbling block.

> The child has little motivation to learn reading and writing when we begin teaching them. He feels no need for them, and has only a vague idea of their usefulness.

Vygotsky's findings are hardly controversial, and yet large numbers of beginning readers are taught by the most abstract and least motivating methods. And because these methods are so intellectually demanding, teachers feel that they have to insist that the children show evidence of sophisticated skills in intellectual analysis and synthesis before teaching of reading can begin.

We have no reason to doubt that the vast majority of children can, before the age of five, *see* all the necessary details in the different letter shapes, or that they can *hear* the differences between all sorts of speech sounds in their mother tongue. The healthy young child has a very good eye and ear for details, but he does not know how to analyse and 'make sense' of all these details. Most beginning readers do not even understand that there is anything to analyse in a conscious, explicit way. They have a highly developed ability to use and to understand language, even fairly complex language. But this ability is entirely *implicit*. Communication functions effectively without the child being aware of *how* if functions, and there is no need for the child to analyse language into its smallest components, to put labels on these components, and then put them all together again. We must therefore not be surprised if, in the field of reading, the children fail to see the need for analysis and synthesis of the 'atoms' of language and find it very difficult to acquire analytic-synthetic skills.

Unfortunately, many teachers find it difficult to accept that teaching of reading *at the beginning stages* has to do without refined, abstract skills of analysis, and synthesis of language. And since these teachers are convinced that analytic-synthetic skills are indispensable, they spend a lot of effort on trying to teach such skills, and never get a chance to discover that children can learn to get meaning from print without these skills.

In Scotland, Jessie Reid (1972) has provided evidence to support Vygotsky's conclusions. Her investigation involved individual interviews with the same group of five-year-old pupils, first after they had attended school for a period of only two months, then after five months and after nine months. Her questions explored the children's concepts, ways of thinking, and attitudes concerning reading. Her findings were:

> For young beginners reading is a mysterious activity, to which they come with only the vaguest of expectations.
>
> They [i.e., the children] displayed a general lack of any specific expectation of
> a) what reading was going to be like;
> b) what the activity consisted of;
> c) the purpose and use of it.
>
> The children had great difficulty in understanding the abstract technical terms in which adults use to talk about language, e.g., "word", "letter", "sound".

Reid's research is being replicated and her findings confirmed in different parts of the world, and one would expect the gradually accumulated evidence to provide guidelines for the initial stages of teaching reading. Children's lack of understanding of the task, and their lack of intrinsic motivation for the task, must surely be aggravated by teaching methods which focus on the most abstract and complex aspects of attaching meaning to print. But education is essentially a conservative field where old habits die hard, and there is often a very wide time lag between educational theory and classroom practice.

Those who swear by the traditional methods are reinforced in their attitudes by the fact that *most* of their pupils do in fact learn to read by these abstract methods. It does not follow, however, that this majority of beginning readers would not make an even better start by the use of less abstract methods of teaching reading. It seems likely that in the long term a meaningful language-based start to reading would result in more desirable attitudes to books and to reading later in life. And the considerable minority of children who fail to make a satisfactory start, and whose progress resembles that of a downward spiral, is probably suffering a great deal from the consequences of too abstract an approach to beginning reading.

When should they start?

The studies cited in support of the view that 'reading readiness begins at six' were mainly American, and many of them dated from the 1920s and 1930s.

It was usually pointed out that reading readiness occurred at a *mental* age of six years, or, as in the much quoted study by Morphett and Washburne (1931): 'it pays to postpone reading until the child has attained a mental age of six years and six months.'

Morphett and Washburne's research was carried out in America and based on observations of 141 children from an environment which was untypically restricted in many respects. This is an interesting example of the idiosyncratic way in which one particular piece of research can have much wider exposure and influence than other studies which from a scientific point of view are equally significant or even more significant. For example, in the same year as the Morphett and Washburne report, Davidson (1931) reported that her experimental group of three–five-year-olds, with a mental age of $4\frac{1}{2}$ years, made considerable progress in reading over a four-month period.

During the same decade Gates (1937) published a study which contradicted the results of Morphett and Washburne. Gates stated:

> it has by no means been proved that a mental age of six and a half years is a proper minimum to prescribe for learning to read by all school methods or organizations or *all* types of teaching skills procedures.

MacGinitie (1969), in a valuable review and evaluation of research in this field, supports Gates' position, and writes:

> it is hazardous to interpret the findings of research studies when the teaching method and materials are not specified.

In other words, the concept of readiness must be related to the teaching methods and materials which are about to be used. A teacher can only make some assessment of a pupil's readiness in specific terms of *what it is that he has to be ready for*.

MacGinitie (1969) also makes the point that the question

> Is the child ready to read?

is, at best, very poorly phrased, since it ignores the long-term developmental nature of reading ability. This ability is acquired gradually over a long period of time, and it is very difficult to point to any particular stage in the process as *the* point where the child changes from a nonreader into a reader. As it stands the question is not sufficiently specific to be meaningful.

Durkin (1970) has suggested that the curiously unquestioning attitude towards the 'rule' that six and a half years mental age is necessary for beginning reading was due to the fact that it was in harmony with popular belief at the time. In American schools pupils enter the first grade at the age of six, and so it is reassuring to believe that they should not make a start in reading until a few months after beginning school. Unfortunately, this belief works out nicely only for the 'average' child whose mental age equals his chronological age. All those children who are below or above average would still have to be treated in a more individual way.

In Scandinavian countries children do not start school until they are seven years old, a tradition which has mainly practical reasons. These countries have widely scattered populations, and many children have to travel long distances to school. But there has been a certain amount of educational rationalization of this tradition, and it is widely believed in Scandinavian countries that children are not 'ready' to learn to read until they are seven years old. It seems, then, as if habits and traditions of schooling have a great influence on beliefs about reading readiness in many parts of the world.

Checklists (often called skills inventories in the USA) are frequently offered to help the teacher to decide whether the right day has arrived on which to begin reading instruction. At best, the questions on these checklists are fairly relevant, relating to the pupil's ability to listen, to follow instructions, to concentrate, etc. But the answers to many of the questions must, in all honesty, be 'Sometimes', 'It depends on what you mean', or 'I don't know'. At worst, these checklists are long lists of only marginally relevant items, demanding an unreasonable degree of observation from a busy classroom teacher, and yielding very little diagnostically useful information.

Teachers in America are less likely to rely upon their own observations or personal judgements than are British teachers. The American approach is much more psychometric, and published tests of 'reading readiness' are widely used. Details of these tests can be found in Buros (1959), Standish (1960), and Pumfrey (1976).

In the USA during the past fifty years, hundreds of studies involving the use of readiness tests have been reported. Attempts to usefully sort and interpret the data collected in all these studies are doomed to failure, because so few studies are in any way comparable. Different populations have been sampled, different variables have been examined, controlled, or ignored, and a wide variety of tests and statistical treatments have been employed. As a consequence, the results pertain to almost as many different kinds of reading readiness as there are studies.

There is, in fact, no evidence to suggest that there exists any set of skills or abilities which are absolutely necessary to master before a child can begin to learn to read. Surprisingly little is known about what is really necessary before a child can learn to read. The skills or characteristics which have been suggested nearly always relate to specific beliefs concerning the nature of the reading task or the method of teaching reading.

In the light of recent research, notably that of Kenneth and Yetta Goodman in the United States, traditional notions about how children should tackle the reading task have had to be rejected or at least considerably revised. (For a summary of their view; see, e.g., Goodman, Goodman, and Burke, 1978.) The traditional notion that, from the very beginning, the aim must be completely error-free reading is, for example, rejected by more and more reading specialists. The same is true of the idea that beginning readers should have a lot of training in analysing words (or parts of words) out of context. The new thinking has, however, been very slow to extend into the area of reading readiness where ideas which are incompatible with current thinking on learning to read and the teaching of reading often prevail.

The Bullock Committee's report, 'A Language for Life' (DES 1975) has been criticized for not giving enough guidance for practical classroom work, but regarding reading readiness the committee has at least made one important unequivocal statement:

> It cannot be emphasized too strongly that the teacher has to help the children toward readiness for beginning reading. There is no question of waiting for readiness to occur, for with many children it does not come 'naturally' and must be brought about by the teacher's positive measures to induce it.

Getting rid of 'readiness'

The confusion, ambiguity, and misrepresentation connected with 'reading readiness' are so entrenched that it would be a good thing if the concept were abandoned altogether. After having noted that the concept of 'reading readiness' has been questioned in recent years, Thackray (1975) formulates the following warning:

> If the concept of reading readiness were abandoned . . . the tendency would

L—2 **

be to start all children on *formal reading* very soon after they entered school. (my italics)

I do agree with Thackray that it seems sensible to 'protect' children from 'formal reading', which has overtones of an inappropriately disciplined and 'intellectualized' approach to learning. But surely there is an unwarranted assumption in this point of view, namely that the beginning stages of reading need to be *'formal'*. Implicit in this viewpoint, which is widely shared, is the notion that reading 'instruction' must of necessity entail the abstract kinds of method discussed earlier in this chapter.

Unfortunately, many teachers view beginning reading as instruction in phonics analysis and as a complex programme of grapheme-phoneme correlations to be recognized and memorized. The training of these abstract skills is often preceded by, or accompanied by, some 'look-and-say' word recognition drill. There is little doubt that the vast majority of children in both the United Kingdom and the United States are confronted by *'formal'* reading instruction, which for many of them may seem like *'formidable'* reading instruction. Many children are not ready *for this kind of approach* to reading at the age of six years, nor at the age of seven or eight years.

Should we, then, take it for granted that a teaching method for which many children are not ready is suitable, and that teaching must be postponed until our pupils are ready to benefit from such a method? Is it not at least equally valid to question the suitability of the method for our young pupils?

How should they begin?

Beginning reading should be *induction* rather than instruction, a gradual introduction of the children into the world of books. Beginning reading should be fun and exciting. Children should be encouraged to *discover* that *print has meaning*, that people write because they have something to say, something children may want to know about. And this process of becoming a reader can be both organized and structured, without any element of 'formal' drill, the meaning of which the children fail to understand.

What we need are guidelines for enabling children to take step after step on the road to reading, and there are some facts that can provide the foundation for such guidelines; for example:

1   *Many children need to be motivated to begin learning to read*

We can achieve this by very carefully selecting a variety of story books to read to the pupils, and to reread to them when requested. Of all the books available in the enormous market, relatively few will be 'winners', and even these books will not be the favourites of *all* pupils. This is why variety is so important. The wider the selection, the more likely it is that *some* of the books will appeal to even the most reluctant listeners and prospective readers.

The stories should be read to the children, and the books should then be made available in the comfortable 'book corner' of the classroom. A resources library of prerecorded cassettes will enable individual pupils to hear their favourite stories as often as they like, while they are looking at the text and beginning to understand what reading is about.

2 *Reading is getting meaning from print*

From this follows that *there must be meaning in the print* which children are offered to read. All the books available to the child should *make sense*, even the early books of reading schemes (basal reading series).

If some of the books in the classroom do not make sense to the children, these books should be thrown out and replaced by books that do make sense, and which have as much appeal for young people as possible. This may seem costly, but there is probably no more profitable way of spending money in the infant school.

It is worth remembering that teachers can become 'immune' to the non-sense in reading books after years of exposure to it. Try to look at a book from the point of view of the pupil who has just started school, and ask yourself if the child is likely to find the text amusing, exciting, interesting, or even meaningful.

come	come	come
come	Tom	come
can	Tom	come?
Tom	can	come

Some of the content of early reading books makes just as much sense if the words are read from right to left instead of from left to right.

It is true that many children learn to read by using books like these, but I fail to see that this justifies their use, particularly since they may have a negative effect on children's interest in books and reading. And of course, there is a considerable minority of children who fail to make adequate progress through these books, and they are are almost certain to grow up with little, if any, interest in books.

3   *Children are individuals*

They have different personalities, temperaments, and learning sets. It is unlikely that every pupil in a class will respond in the same way to one and the same teaching method, or that every pupil will progress at the same steady rate of learning.

Beginning reading materials should be organized into levels of difficulty, but there should be plenty of options at each level. If records are kept for each pupil, his progress can be monitored, and it can be ensured that he is tackling, at each level, books, games, and other materials which *he is enjoying*. He should be experiencing success as often as possible, and gaining self-confidence in the process. Reading should become an exciting game, and he should know that it is fun to play and that he is good at it.

4   *Young children are not attracted to abstract concepts*

It makes sense to avoid initial approaches to teaching reading which focus on abstract concepts like individual 'letter sounds', blends, etc. Instead, teaching should begin by using the children's *own* experiences and language. The teacher should print what a pupil wants to say about a painting, a new toy, the class hamster, etc., and build up for him a personal reading book which he can share with other children. Personal reading books should be kept carefully and reread regularly.

5   *Reading is a language activity*

Reading is firmly rooted in language, along with listening, speaking, and writing. The more practised a child is in spoken language, the more easily he will understand written language. It follows that the development of spoken language must have very high priority in early schooling. This can be achieved in a number of ways, and some of these ways provide the focal point for the language and reading curriculum described later in this book.

Improving spoken language is a valuable activity in its own right, but it also prepares children for learning to get meaning from written language – that is, for reading.

School teaching for literacy beings in the nursery class

In the DES pamphlet 'Progress in Education' (1978) it is reported that between 1974 and 1978 the number of children in nursery schools and classes in England rose from 125,000 to over 200,000, and that in addition to this there were, in 1975, 315,000 children under five years in infant classes in primary schools. This growth in the nursery sector is a very important feature of current educational change. It is generally agreed that it is beneficial for children to attend nursery classes, but there is surprisingly little discussion or debate concerning the aims of nursery education. There are four main reasons for this:

1 insufficient focus on the nursery years for educational growth

2 too little differentiation between education and 'baby-minding'

3 neglect of the nursery years in educational research

4 widespread confusion about the notion of 'readiness' to learn.

A BBC survey in 1975 yielded the information that less than one-fifth of the nursery teachers involved listed intellectual growth or language development among the aims of their work. A cautious and restrictive attitude to learning of any kind at nursery level is fairly widespread. The real losers in the 'waiting for readiness' game so often played in our schools are the children whose environment does not provide adequate opportunities for the development of those aspects of language that are particularly important in school. A child may be highly intelligent, but severely handicapped by not having heard or used very much language of the kind needed for school during his preschool years. It must be emphasized that his handicap is not 'lack of language', since practically all children are quite sophisticated language-users when they come to school. The handicap is lack of the kind of language that facilitates entry into the world of written language.

If a child with this kind of handicap finds himself in what Lancaster and Gaunt (1976) describe as 'the strange wordless world of the nursery school', he will be quite unprepared for infant school. If his infant schoolteacher then waits for his mythical 'teachable moment', and eventually feels she cannot wait any longer and *begins* to teach him the most abstract features of the reading process, then his chances of success are slim indeed. Such a child may soon be labelled 'dull', 'remedial', or 'retarded'. In many cases the label in the school record should read 'victim of bad teaching'. If retardation follows, it may have been aggravated, perhaps even caused, by excessive waiting for 'readiness' instead of actively helping the child to develop it.

The view of *readiness for reading* upon which this approach to reading and the teaching of reading is based can be summarized in one simple question and one even simpler answer:

Question: When is a nursery/infant child ready to take
             the next step in his development towards
             literacy?

Answer: Now.

And the way to take the first steps towards literacy is by *induction*, not instruction.

CHAPTER 3

THE DEVELOPMENT OF LANGUAGE SKILLS

There should be positive steps to develop the language ability of children in the pre-school and nursery and infant years . . .

'A Language for Life'
(HMSO 1975)

The language of young children

Templin (1957) in the USA carried out a comprehensive study of the relationships of language skills in preschool children to those of primary school children. In her study she applied a longitudinal approach and selected 490 children who provided representative groups in terms of parental occupation, age, sex, and IQ. From the results of periodic testing and observation, Templin demonstrated a progressive change along with age in the mean scores gained by children in vocabulary tests, as well as in the total number of words used at successive age levels.

This study is one of several which indicate that children's command of vocabulary increases progressively from one developmental stage to another. But this increase is not a universally consistent phenomenon since it is dependent upon a combination of factors which do not prevail equally for all children.

Joan Tough's recent studies (1974, 1976) point explicitly towards the differences between the language experience which a child may have in what she calls an 'educating home' and that which characterizes a home which is markedly less 'educating'. Chapter Three of Joan Tough's *Focus of Meaning* gives illustrations of different kinds of spoken communication between mother and child. The importance of the preschool years in the development of language skills is now generally acknowledged among educationists. It is also widely accepted that during the primary school period, which in the UK represents the age range from five to twelve years, children go through a stage of language development which is next in importance to the preschool period. In spite of a considerable volume of research (for recent reviews see, e.g., Cazden 1969, Day 1974, and Pearce 1975) our knowledge about the language of young children and its development is still far from complete. In the preschool child, language learning seems to be largely incidental. Language used by children and by adults communicating with children is mainly instrumental – an integrated part of acting and interacting. In the words of Bellugi-Klima (1970), who has analysed a wide variety of parent-child conversations:

> The mother and child are concerned with daily activities, not grammatical instruction . . .

> Neither of the two seems overtly concerned with the problems that we . . . pursue so avidly: the acquisition of syntax.

Slobin (1968) has found that a mother's utterances to her child are both shorter and simpler than her utterances to another adult. But there is no evidence of parents sequencing what the child has to learn (Cazden 1969). The structure of the language to be learned cannot be expressed in grammatic concepts; this structure is rather determined by the situation in which language is used, by the relationship between the persons communicating – the child and the adult – and by the needs and interests of the child. Weir (1962) has offered the simile of the child being offered a rich *a la carte* menu rather than a carefully prescribed linguistic diet. From this 'menu' the child takes what he needs in order to build gradually his own language system, geared to his particular purpose of communication. This is, of course, only possible if the 'menu' contains, among all its different items, things that appeal to the individual child. As Cazden (*op. cit.*) has pointed out:

> All that the child needs is exposure to well-formed sentences in the context of conversation that is *meaningful and sufficiently personally important to command attention*. (my italics)

On the basis of her research into the language acquisition of schoolchildren (aged six to ten years) Carol Chomsky (1972) comes to a similar conclusion. She points out that:

> We know very little about the actual processes by which children learn language, but there has been an increasing awareness over the past few years of just how much the child brings to the task by way of his own internal organization and innate human characteristics. He certainly is not 'taught' language in any formal sense, but acquires it naturally, so to speak, in the course of maturing and devloping *in an enviornment where he is adequately exposed to it* . . . this natural process of acquisition continues actively into the early school years, and perhaps beyond. (*op. cit.*, my italics)

A child's language can be seen as developing organically out of his interaction with the environment and with the people in the environment. However, as the quotations from Cazden (1969) and Chomsky (1972) above show, this does not mean that the development of a child's language can be left entirely to 'nature'. The actual processes of learning language need not be sequenced and organized for young children, but their opportunities for involvement in processes that further language learning may very usefully be systematically planned and organized.

If we want to make sure that a child's immediate environment presents a sufficient variety of communicative opportunities, we would have to start by analysing the uses of language that are most important in the lives of children.

Halliday (1969) has tried to outline various functions of language which are relevant to the uses children actually make of language. He identifies the following functions and describes them in terms of the child's intentions:

Instrumental function – the 'I want' function, where language is used for the satisfaction of material needs;

Regulatory function – the 'do as I tell you' function, using language for control of behaviour;

Personal function – the 'here I come' function, where language expresses and establishes identiy, largely through linguistic interaction with others;

Heuristic function – the 'tell me why' function of learning and exploration of reality;

Imaginative function – the 'let's pretend' function which creates new reality; and, finally,

Representational function – the 'I've got something to tell you' function of the communication of content.

Halliday (*op. cit.*) points out that some of these language functions are more crucial to educational success than others. The representational function, for example, is the predominant one in many school situations, although it may be one of the less important functions for the child personally.

It is doubtful whether Halliday's model of language functions provides a fully satisfactory classificatory scheme, since there must be a great deal of overlap between functions (e.g., between the instrumental and the regulatory), and since language usage may have several functions simultaneously (e.g., representational, interactional, and personal). A criticism of Halliday's and other models is provided by Wight (1978), who also proposes his own alternative model. Halliday's list seems, however, to have great heuristic value in that it emphasizes the richness of linguistic functions available to a child. If we are aware of the many uses of language, we will find it easier to understand that language can be different things to different people; and particularly that language has not necessarily the same function for the child as it has for the adult.

A large body of recent research on the language of young children has been critically reviewed and summarized by Day (1974). He makes the distinction between 'language competence' and 'language maturity', and concludes from his review that language competence develops from an innate, biological base and is 'a fairly universal occurrence. It is rare and unusal when someone doesn't exhibit it; status, intelligence, culture are all insignificant variables' (*op. cit.*). Language maturity, on the other hand, is a later, gradual process which is very much dependent upon the environment. In Day's words:

> A child's language can begin to mature only after control of the basic rules of the language [i.e., language competence in Day's terminology] has been achieved. Once this occurs, the demands individuals and situations make on the child . . . will provoke development. . . . Language can be explicit or it can be vague and ambiguous. The degree to which it is either will reflect the stimulation and encouragement children receive in their use of language to organize and describe their behaviour. (*op. cit.*)

Day accepts, as do many linguists and educators, Chomsky's (1957, 1965) view of language development as mainly determined by some innate capacity, and not resulting from attempts to imitate adult speech (the view held, for example, by Skinner 1957). Day's distinction between competence and maturity (see above) seems very much to be a terminological artefact, invented for the purposes of reconciling Chomsky's 'innateness hypothesis' with the empirical evidence, suggesting that 'language matures in response to social stimuli' (Day, *op. cit.*).

Day's competence-maturity dichotomy may well be a misleading dichotomy, since it is hard to imagine a point in the language development before which the child does not 'respond to social stimuli', but after which he does respond to them. In spite of the somewhat unfortunate attempt at 'terminological reform', it is, in my opinion, easy to sympathize with Day's position, which in very simple terms boils down to answering the old 'nature *or* nurture' question with a firm 'nature *and* nuruture' answer. This is not the place for detailed discussion of the intricacies of the Skinner versus Chomsky debate concerning the origin of language. But it is worth pointing out that a position like the one advocated by Day is a merger of a developmental view and a modified behaviourist view – one might even call it a *'socio-behaviourist'* view.

This 'nature *and* nurture' view of language development is not only compatible with empirical evidence, it is also pedagogically valuable, since it emphasizes the need for the teacher to be sensitive both to the potentialities and to the limitations of children's innate capacity for language, and to provide the 'social stimuli' necessary for optimal language development.

Language competence and its assessment

Linguistic competence has been defined by Chomsky (1965) as *the abstraction underlying language performance*. Accepting the assumption that 'competence' is a variable pertaining to an *actual* rather than an *idealized* speaker, how can we test linguistic performance in such a way as to measure competence? A possible solution is not to allow the child to talk at will, but to present him with a situation that will stretch his competence to the fullest. Accepting the unavoidable constraints on a child in a test situation of this nature, the task would appear to be an almost impossible one.

Labov (1970), studying the speech fluency of black American children, claims that the stress which is imposed by the experimental situation in general, and the 'socio-ethnic' difference between interviewer and interviewee (i.e., the pupil), may seriously impair performance of the interviewee on any task given to him with the aim of measuring his spoken language competence. Even if the 'socio-ethnic' differences are not as great and as obvious as those between a white 'middle-class' teacher and a black 'working-class' child in an American city, they can still be sufficiently great to interfere with the child's performance in a language test situation.

Brown (1973) has written a searching analysis of the semantic and syntactic aspects of the language development of the preschool child. In his conclusion, he refers to the difficulties involved in establishing what may or may not be a child's linguistic competence. He predicts:

> We shall find, I think, that there are multiple 'levels' of knowledge of structure, as revealed by various kinds of performance, and that there is no clear reason to enthrone any one of these as the child's true competence. Some aspects of linguistic knowledge, as revealed in regularities of spontaneous speech, will not, I suspect, ever attain the judgemental level in the naive speaker. Prominent among these, perhaps, are the kind of probabilities that Labov has found it necessary to enter into the rules describing Black English and other dialects. Beyond the level of judgement and correction is the level of rule formulation, and this is a level attained only by people who study linguistics.

One area of linguistic development that has been investigated involves the amount and rate of linguistic expression as well as the complexity and length of the child's verbal responses. In studying these aspects, many researchers have utilized an approach which consists of a quantitative measurement of the *'amount'* of children's speech. This approach, according to McCarthy (1954), provides objective data which can be easily scored in relation to both the length of verbal responses and the number or frequency of words used by a child at any given age. Yet, she adds, it does not refer 'to the quality of the expression or to any details of the complexities of sentence structure'. Associated with these limitations are certain problems which the investigator has to take into account when tabulating the number and frequency of words used by children under study. These include the variety of root and derivative words used, the different meanings of words which the child may employ in a given context, and the exclusion or inclusion of terms like proper nouns, verb forms, and coined words. In view of these problems, many researchers are of the opinion that results yielded by quantitative measurements lack validity, especially during the primary school years when the qualitative aspects of speech become increasingly important.

In his review of research on oral language and reading, Weintraub (1968) found that a number of studies did not reveal any particularly high correlations between measures of oral language skills, on the one hand, and measures of reading skills, on the other. One of Weintraub's main conclusions was 'that measures of fluency in oral language may be inadequate'.

Fleming (1968) who agrees with Weintraub regarding the inadequacy of most measures of oral language proficiency, points to one, in his opinion, very important cause of this inadequacy:

> Instruments used to obtain indices of linguistic maturity in children are basically inadequate if they incorporate only such items as number of sentences, number of words, length of sentences, type-token ratios, and the like. One reason these instruments are basically inadequate is because of their total neglect of syntax . . . any instrument which purports to measure language development in children must include some means of taking into account . . . the way in which his language performance is structured. (*op. cit.*)

Several researchers (e.g., Loban 1963, McCarthy 1954, Templin 1957) have attempted to assess language competence through observation of children's language errors. Obviously, the competent user of a language should be expected to use it correctly, i.e., according to commonly accepted rules of grammar. The problem with this approach to the assessment of language competence is that not all rules of grammar are universally adopted even by adult users of a language. Some children commit errors not because they lack language competence but because their language is partly governed by other grammatic rules than those accepted among educated adults in general and teachers in particular. If the assessment of language competence is based on children's errors, what was meant to be a measure of a child's ability to use language for various communicative purposes may instead become a measure of the degree to which he has mastered the rules of Standard English. This is not to say that there is no need for assessing children's mastery of Standard English, only that the two purposes of assessment must not be confused.

Carol Chomsky (1972) did find a positive correlation between assessment of the stage of children's linguistic competence on the one hand, and various reading indices on the other. Her reading variables were, however, more concerned with the frequency and amount of children's reading than with their reading performance. And although her study involved schoolchildren (aged six to ten years), the tests she used cannot be regarded as suitable for classroom use. She tested children's ability to understand phrases like 'easy to see' as compared to 'eager to see', i.e., phrases involving rather subtle – and somewhat contrived – nuances of prepositional meaning.

Chomsky is aware of this herself and cautions her readers

> against considering these constructions relevant for practical purposes such as diagnostic procedures or for teaching to children. (*op. cit.*)

An interesting attempt to devise scales for the assessment of language development has been made by Reynell and Huntley (1971). Having found no suitable scales covering the age range from one to five years, they decided to develop their own scales in response to the needs at a centre for handicapped children. Two scales, 'Verbal Comprehension' and 'Expressive Language', were devised and standardized on a sample of about 650 children in southeast England. The scales have, according to the author's report, sufficient reliability for use as diagnostic tools. However, little is known about their validity. In particular, no data seems to be available which indicate their predictive validity, for example, for the purpose of predicting language development in the infant school on the basis of pre-school data. Since the scales concentrate on assessing language development in children between the ages of one and a half and four years, they cannot be used in studies of infant school children (aged five to seven years).

In an attempt to measure language competence and to compare competence scores with scores of various aspects of reading attainment, Gill (1971) devised a 'Language Production' test which included four subtests involving the production of restrictive relative clauses analysed as identifying descriptions. She concluded that the test could not be considered as a good measure of linguistic competence, since so many extraneous variables appear to have affected children's performance on the test.

This review of the problems of linguistic competence shows that there is a conspicuous lack of instruments which are suitable for use in practical classroom situations. Some tests are not regarded as suitable even by their authors (e.g., Gill 1971), and other tests are mainly suitable for research purposes (Chomsky 1972). In a study of the effects of an experimental language and reading programme for the infant school, it seems, therefore, more useful to concentrate on the assessment of reading ability on the assumption that improvement in a child's ability to use language will manifest itself in – among other things – improvement in his reading ability, i.e., in his ability to understand or make meaning from written language.

Improving language skills in school

Systematic classroom work which has as its primary aim the improvement of infant school children's spoken language skills is rarely encountered in the United Kingdon. Perhaps it is commonly assumed that children will be fluent and articulate in their speech depending upon variables such as intelligence, temperament, home and environmental influences, etc. Certainly in the vast majority of schools the task of improving the articulateness of the pupils would be viewed as an incidental objective of the curriculum rather than as a direct one.

Even where the improvement of the pupil's spoken language is recognized as an objective of schooling the pupil-teacher ratio usually limits the amount of one-to-one communication which is possible in the school day. The busy infant school teacher finds it difficult to hear individual pupils reading as often as she considers necessary, and she also has to provide instruction in other areas of the curriculum.

It is not suggested here that the *incidental* communication at a one-to-one level has no value in improving the pupil's spoken language ability. On the contrary, it is greatly beneficial and has the merit of usually arising from the immediate needs and interests of the child. What is questionable is whether incidental teaching to improve spoken language skills is *sufficient* provision in this fundamentally important area. For a fortunate minority of children, this provision may be adequate. Some children have frequent opportunities to communicate with articulate adults (parents and others), and have learned to use language in those functions which are particularly important in education (*cf.* discussion above of Halliday's models of language use). These children should require little training, direct or incidental, in the use of language for the normal purposes of classroom communication. But because these children have no real *problems* in communicating, it does not follow that no benefits would be derived from positive attempts to improve or extend the language skills even of this privileged minority.

It would be difficult to estimate the ratio of children from 'educating homes' to 'disadvantaged' children in this respect. In any case, no clear dividing line exists between the two categories, but there is, rather, a *continuum* of levels of experience and degrees of linguistic sophistication. But, clearly, some children are less fortunate than others in their home backgrounds vis-à-vis language experience, and for these I suggest that an incidental approach to spoken language development is insufficient. At the far end of the 'disadvantaged' continuum are children whose parents, family, and friends speak no English, and who converse at home in a language other than English.

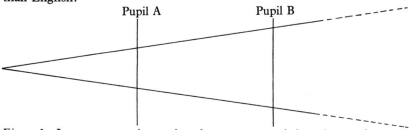

Figure 1 Language experience viewed as an open-ended *continuum*, for crude 'measurement'.

The deficit-difference controversy

It would be inaccurate and misleading to suggest that these children, who do not communicate in English outside school, are 'deprived' or 'disadvantaged' in their early language development and experience. They may well be listening to and becoming familiar with very rich and stimulating language. But these 'tools of communication', however many and varied, are not the ones which are used in the school system. The five-year-old from a non-English-speaking home must surely feel 'disadvantaged' when the language used by his teacher and the majority of his fellow pupils is a language which he cannot understand or use. Even if all adults who are responsible for his education fully understand that this child is *not deficient in language*, but that his language is *different*, it seems to me that, for the child himself, there is little consolation in the distinction. Those first weeks in school during which the 'different' child must rapidly learn to express his ideas in an entirely new language can only be bewildering at best, and frightening at worst.

A similar, but less extreme, difference exists in the kind of language heard and used by children from widely different socio-economic groups within our native population. Some children, during their preschool years, listen to and learn to use a kind of English which is different from the kind of English used by their teacher when they go to school. Without making any unnecessary value judgements about which kind of English is best or better, it must be accepted that the teacher's English is the one which prevails, and that this is the kind of English which is widely accepted as the 'standard language' of our society.

If new pupils are not familiar with the teacher's language usage, they will be required to adapt to a certain degree – or else remain to some extent inhibited or handicapped in their communication. They may be highly intelligent and full of ideas, but *their* language, is not the one that is favoured in the school situation. This is a problem which is surrounded by a great many emotionally and politically determined attitudes, some of which border on hypocrisy. It is often referred to as the *difference-deficit* question, underlining the fact that it is unfair and misleading to imply that children have a *'language deficit'* when they may have splendid powers of expression in a language which is merely *'different'*.

It is not only desirable, but essential, that the difference-deficit problem is appreciated by all educationists. But this understanding should not lead to complacency, or to neglect of the educational implications of the 'language difference'. While recognizing and acknowledging that a child's spoken language is not 'deficient' simply because it is 'different', his teachers should not fail to appreciate that the 'difference' is likely to constitute an inhibiting factor in the child's ability to communicate in certain situations. And as the child attempts to modify his 'different' language according to the demands of the school situation, his ability to communicate may be temporarily hampered and slowed down. Even if the teacher is careful not to put any undue pressure on the child with a language difference in order to make him 'conform', the very fact that the child's language is different may create such a pressure.

In the USA, during the 1960s, there were several experimental attempts to reduce the handicap in language usage experienced by children from the lower socio-economic groups. These are known as compensatory education programmes, one of the most publicized being the one developed by Bereiter and Engelmann (1966). The concept of 'conpensatory education' is criticized by Bernstein in an article entitled 'Education cannot compensate for society' (1972). He claims that the term 'compensatory', in this context, implies that the educational system is satisfactory, and that it is certain families, and hence certain children, who are thought of as 'deficit systems', in need of 'compensatory' education. Bernstein argues that it is the education system which is deficient in meeting the needs of a large section of the population in our society. The concept of compensatory education for pupils who are 'disadvantaged' or 'deprived' implies that our education system is sound but that the children, *for whom it does not cater*, are at fault. He points out the dangers of labelling children 'deprived' or 'disadvantaged'. There is a body of research evidence pointing to the likelihood that teacher expectations can influence pupil performance, and Bernstein claims that because of this process 'these labels do their own sad work'.

While agreeing with Bernstein in his criticism of the deficiencies of the current education system, one can still make the point that 'compensatory' education *can* be seen as an attempt to provide compensation for the deficiencies in the system rather than in the child. Our education system is essentially conservative, and no fundamental change is likely to be implemented in the near future. Until such time as the system is changed so that it caters properly for all groups of children, a case could be made for making some attempts, albeit piecemeal, to remedy some of the negative effects of our present, deficient system. And there is no doubt about it that it may be much easier – and quicker – to provide an additional provision for groups not catered for in the present system than to change the normal provision throughout the whole system.

The performance-competence controversy

Labov (1970) has shown that black American children, who appeared to have limited language ability when tested by a white adult, gave evidence of much more fluent language ability when tested by a black adult in a more relaxed situation. This supports the belief that most of the test procedures used in the field of language are culture-dependent. Tests used to measure, for example, IQ or reading ability are usually designed by white Anglo-Saxon Protestants (WASPs) for children who belong to this dominant cultural group, and who are consequently at an advantage in the test situations, compared to black children, chicano children, the children of American Indians, and many other minority groups in the American society.

This test or measurement problem as it relates to language and culture is closely connected with the performance-competence controversy. This term underlines the fact that a child's language *competence*, i.e., his potential language ability, may be far greater than his *performance* in situations where constraints are operating. The distinction between competence, as the knowledge of language that might under ideal circumstances be utilized, and performance, as the language ability that is *de facto* utilized in a given situation, is a very useful one, and one which all educationists should be aware of. It must be remembered, however, that language competence can never be directly observed or assessed. The only thing we can observe and assess is language performance in a variety of situations, and from the performance we can try to make inferences concerning the competence. It is also worth pointing out that it is, in practice, usually performance that 'counts'. There is little consolation for a pupil to have high competence, when he perhaps lacks the confidence or experience to realize his potential in actual performance.

Awareness of the possibility of a considerable gap between competence and performance should help the teacher to explore and initiate curriculum innovations with the aim of reducing the gap as far as possible. Bernstein (1972) argues that the child's own form of language should be accepted in school, and should not be corrected by the teacher and reflected back to the child as 'inferior language'. Bernstein makes the point that it is generally accepted educational practice to begin with what the child brings – the known and familiar – to the educational situation, and he asks why so many teachers do not do so when it comes to language.

While it certainly makes sense to 'start where the child is' in the case of language, there are a number of other factors which the class teacher must take into account:

a) the great majority of teachers do not, and cannot, speak in a language form other than that of the higher socio-economic groups, i.e., mainly 'middle-class' language;

b) the great majority of people value certain language forms more highly than others, and the most highly valued forms of language are to a large extent associated with the middle class;

c) many teachers, implicitly, if not explicitly, view 'improvement' of their pupils' language forms as an important part of their task as teachers, and such 'improvement' often means change in the direction of 'middle-class' language;

d) many parents would support class teachers in this aim, since they regard language 'improvement', rightly or wrongly, as a means of upward social mobility in the children's careers after school.

Educational implications

To reject the 'deficit' argument in favour of a 'difference' argument in the field of language development does not solve the educational problems faced by the children concerned. To say that these children are not 'deficient', and leave it at that, would be far too complacent, as long as nursery and infant schools throughout the United Kingdom enrol large numbers of children into classes where the language environment is alien to the experience of these children.

A young child's first encounters with the world of school need to be handled with sympathy and care. I would suggest that the child's basic communication system, the language through which his initiation is achieved, is central to the success of these encounters. The language which the child hears in school should be one with which he is 'at home', and certainly one which he can understand and use without effort and embarrassment.

In order to achieve this, schools need to recruit intelligent, sympathetic adults whose language is similar to that of the newly arrived nursery or infant pupils, whether this be a language other than English or a nonstandard variety of English. If the cost of training and paying the salaries of a sufficient number of teacher aides proves prohibitive, experience has shown that many mothers are happy to fulfil this role on a voluntary part-time basis, guided and supervised by class teachers. In fact, many infant schools already enjoy regular and valuable assistance from volunteer mothers. They help in a variety of ways, from making teaching materials to supervising classroom activities, and, in some cases, helping in the work of developing the pupils' language skills.

The familiar language with which the new pupils would be met and initiated into school life would undoubtedly ease those first, bewildering days at school, and should help to develop in the pupils positive attitudes towards school and learning. The child should feel that he 'belongs', and then his confidence in his ability to cope with this new life is likely to grow. As he encounters new friends, toys, and educational materials and equipment, his vocabulary will grow and his language should develop in pace with the growth of concepts and ideas. Gradually, he will come to understand and accept the fact that all people do not speak alike.

As long as the child's own language expression is not rejected or corrected, he will come to know that there are different ways of saying things, and that if he wants to be able to communicate with the people around him, he may have to learn new ways of expressing himself. His teachers, while making great efforts to express themselves in ways which the child can understand, will be setting examples of spoken English which will become part of the child's education.

Education is, after all, a widening of experience. It is what Peters (1971) defines as 'initiation into what is worthwhile'.

Most teachers would put clarity of expression high on the list of worthwhile objectives for their pupils, and spoken language development should be an important component of the curriculum for *all* nursery and infant pupils.

Clearly, the development of any skill benefits from *practice*, and the view taken here is that all children of infant school age would derive benefit from more practice in language communication. While incidental practice may suffice for some children, I believe that the majority would derive benefit from a curriculum which sets out to meet specific objectives *in a systematic way*.

On the basis of an extensive review of the relevant research, Day (1974) formulates propositions of which teachers should be mindful as they contemplate oral language curricula:

> Oral language must focus on the inter-relatedness of thought and speech
> . . .
>
> Children should be given extensive opportunity in developing skills in using their language in *description, organization, speculation* and inquiry
> . . .
>
> Teachers must attend to the children's language development . . .
>
> I can think of nothing more important for a teacher of young children to do than to provide for each child's use of his language in significant interaction each day. (*op. cit.*)

And Barnes (1971) emphasizes the need for language by using it in real, personal communcation:

> To put it bluntly, too many children spend too much time vaguely listening and then regurgitating: throughout the curriculum they should be required to use language for playing with stories and ideas, for exploring things and people, and sometimes for organizing thought and feeling explicitly. *And this will require teachers to use more inventively the linguistic possibilities of the classroom.* (my italics)

The improvement of spoken language skills requires no further justification on general educational grounds, but language skills also have a special dimension of importance as they relate to reading skills. The relationship between language skills and reading ability has for a long time been recognized by educators. For example, Hildreth (1958) and Templin (1957) have suggested that children with reading problsm are deficient in their language skills. And more recently a school of psycholinguists claims that a child's level of competence in spoken language may be an important contributory factor in his ability to read. Smith (1971) writes:

> reading is an aspect of language only superficially different from the comprehension of speech and . . . many of the skills employed by a child in learning the regularities of spoken language may also be employed to learn reading.

If, from the beginning, reading is viewed as a set of skills by which a child derives meaning from written communication, it follows that his skill in understanding and using spoken communication will contribute to his progress and development as a reader. In particular, psycholinguistic 'guessing-game' techniques depend largely upon the reader's familiarity with the structures, patterns, and rhythms of spoken language which enable him to make intelligent guesses about the likely meaning of unknown words. It is, therefore, with the specific intention of improving reading ability (as well as for its own intrinsic value) that emphasis on spoken language development should be given top priority at nursery and infant school levels, and indeed throughout the years of schooling.

Today's psycholinguistic view of reading has provided us with a better basis for understanding the relationship between language and reading, but educators of an earlier generation have demonstrated this understanding. For example, as early as 1936 an elementary school inspector in Chicago wrote an article in *Childhood Education* entitled 'Implications of Language in Beginning Reading'. She advocated systematic, organized efforts towards language development:

> The entire development of language skills implied in introductory reading cannot be left to individual, unorganized opportunities. . . . In order to be sure that each child is having the training for his particular needs and to keep track of his growth, some more organized procedures are necessary. (Adams 1936)

The insight into the need to promote language development along with reading development is, then, not new. But it is my belief that this insight has not, as yet, sufficiently influenced classroom practice in many of our nursery and infant schools.

CHAPTER 4
TEACHER SKILLS—PUPIL SKILLS

What makes a good teacher?

> Reading failure is due to poor eyesight, or a nervous stomach, or poor posture, or heredity, or a broken home, or undernourishment, or a wicked step-mother, or an Oedipus complex, or sibling rivalry, or God knows what . . . never the school or the teacher.

Flesch, *Why Johnny Can't Read* (1955)

Flesch wrote his book, *Why Johnny Can't Read*, in protest against what he considered to be unprofessional, unsystematic, 'laissez-faire' practice in American primary schools during the 1920s and 1930s. The book condemns the passive or negative nature of the teachers' role in many 'progressive' schools of the period, and it emphasizes the crucial importance of what the school does – mainly through the teacher – to help the children to learn to read.

One of the most commonly noted factors in research on reading is the importance of the teacher's ability as an instructor or as a 'facilitator' of learning (for a review of research particularly relating to teacher behaviour in reading, see e.g., Emans and Fox 1973). The vital role played by the teacher is not, of course, specific to the field of reading. A large number of studies into teaching and the roles of teachers have emphasized this importance in the educational field in general. This extensive research may not have yielded much insight into what makes a 'good' teacher good, but it has provided many confirmations of the importance of teacher's influence on pupil learning (for summaries of research in this field, see e.g., Goldberg 1967, Gage 1972, Medley 1972, and Dunkin and Biddle 1974).

Numerous attempts have been made to identify the most important characteristics of a good teacher. Most writers seem to prefer to provide their own list of skills and characteristics, but there is a great deal of overlap in that one and the same aspect of teaching skill (or highly similar aspects) is often given different names. One interesting attempt to list 'main pedagogical abilities' has been made by the Soviet educationist, N.V. Kusmina. Her list has the advantage of seeming to be fairly 'neutral' with regard to teaching style, so that even educators who differ in their view of what is the best teaching style would probably agree about the importance of Kusmina's main abilities, which are as follows:

a)   power of observation

b)   imagination

c)   tactfulness

d)   high sense of duty, applicable both to oneself and others

e)   distributive attention

f)   organizing ability.

(Kusmina 1963)

Curriculum can perhaps most simply be described as the *specification* of the education to be given to a particular category of pupils in a particular school or school system. In the same vein, teaching can be described as the implementation of the curriculum. From this it follows that an important aspect of teaching skills is the ability to work according to a plan, towards an explicitly defined goal. This 'pedagogical ability' is not mentioned in Kusmina's list, but it is closely related to the sixth ability on her list, 'organizing ability'. The question of how teachers and their teaching behaviour can be influenced is of great importance in the development and implementation of a curriculum, in reading as well as in any other field. Unfortunately, most of the 'pedagogical abilities' listed by Kusmina seem to be character traits which are deeply rooted in the personality of the teacher candidate and which cannot easily be influenced during the normal course of teacher training. Furthermore, the development in an individual of such qualities as imagination, sense of duty, and power of observation is an elusive aim, the achievement of which is difficult to ascertain.

It seems to me that it is in the field of what Kusmina calls 'organizing ability' – and the related ability to work according to a plan – that the most positive contribution can be made. Although teachers may have more or less 'natural' talent for organizing classroom work, many organizing skills are sufficiently tangible and observable to be both taught and assessed in the course of initial or 'inservice' teacher training. It must be emphasized that 'organizing ability' here refers to goal-oriented, 'responsive' ability to organize classroom work. A teacher working according to a detailed plan which does not take into account the needs of individual children in the class is not showing any true organizing ability, at least not one which is educationally valid and relevant. Kusmina is clearly aware of this need for flexible and 'responsive' organization, since she writes:

> The ability of a teacher to rearrange his work in accordance with changed demands, and with regard to the individual peculiarities of children, is proof of his creative capacity. (*op. cit.*)

In an attempt to identify some guidelines which might be useful in the planning and preparation of school courses, P.H. Taylor (1970) undertook a research project investigating teachers' planning and organization of their work. The findings about his sample of teachers were as follows:

a)   they showed lack of confidence in describing how their courses were planned;

b)   they did not employ shared technical experience;

c)   they appeared unable to discuss principles and terms of reference;

d)   they emphasized aims and subject matter rather than teaching methods, the standard to be achieved and procedures of evaluation;

e)   they were aware of complexities, but they had no systematic approach to dealing with them.

These findings do not refer specifically to the planning of courses in the teaching of reading, but their implications for this field are worth considering. It is significant that the three principal recommendations stated by Taylor urge teachers to devise a *policy* which is *organized* and *systematic*.

Helping teachers to develop their ability to organize classroom work and to work towards specified goals is, then, an important part of the attempt to implement a curriculum. The complexity of the teacher's role in society now, and the many pressures imposed by the job of teaching, add weight to the importance of knowing how to improve the teacher's organizing and planning ability. The most obvious way of trying to do this is by improving the curriculum, i.e., the specification of what the teaching is expected to convey to the children. But teachers also need to have access to methods and materials which enable them to work towards the goals specified in the curriculum. These aspects of the development and implementation of a curriculum in reading will be discussed in the following sections of this chapter.

Aims and objectives for teaching and learning reading

The conclusion of the Bullock Committee (DES 1975) that there is no one method which 'holds the key to the process of learning to read' has already been quoted above, and it has also been pointed out that this does not mean that all methods must be considered equally good. Each method must, therefore, be evaluated, and this evaluation must relate the outcome of the method to certain educational objectives, in this case objectives in the field of reading.

As there are different opinions regarding what methods should be employed in teaching reading, so there are different views of what the objectives of this teaching are. In its most simple formulation, the objective of the teaching of reading is to develop in the learner the ability to read. This objective is, however, far too general to provide any guidance for the teaching. Before any more specific objectives can be deduced or developed, an attempt must be made to identify the major features of the reading process, and of the process of learning to read. Such attempts have been made by several reading experts. One of the most successful is, in my opinion, the set of 'principles of teaching reading' formulated by Heilman (1972). The principles are listed here in a slightly amended version:

1   Learning to read is a complicated process, and is sensitive to a variety of pressures. Too much pressure or the wrong kind of pressure may result in nonlearning.

2   Learning to read is an individual process.

3   Pupil differences must be a primary consideration in reading instruction.

4   Reading instruction should be thought of as an organized, systematic, growth-producing activity.

5   Proper reading instruction depends upon the diagnosis of each child's weaknesses and needs.

6   The best diagnosis is pointless unless it is used as a basis for instruction.

7   No child should be expected or forced to attempt to read material which, at the time, he is incapable of reading.

8   Reading is a process of getting meaning from printed word symbols. It is not merely a process of making conventionalized noises associated with these symbols.

9   Any given technique, practice, or procedure is likely to work better with some children than with others. Hence, the teacher must have a variety of approaches.

10   Learning to read is a long-term, developmental process extending over a period of years.

A set of basic principles of this kind constitutes a framework for the formulation of objectives for the teaching of reading, which are specific enough to guide direct efforts of teaching and learning. The tenth and last of Heilman's principles listed above is probably the most important of them all, particularly if linked with the insight that reading development is interwoven with other aspects of language development. If reading is deriving meaning from written language, then it is obvious that reading development cannot precede language development. That is, a child cannot be expected to read language which he cannot understand.

The objectives of the reading curriculum must, consequently, be developed within the framework of a wider curriculum for language development, so as to ensure that what the child is expected to achieve in reading is commensurate with his general language development.

The educational objectives controversy

Since there are widely differing opinions about the usefulness of educational objectives in education, a few words about the nature of objectives may be useful here. Proponents of an educational technology approach usually insist on the formulation of *behavioural objectives*. Rowntree (1974), for example, makes a distinction between aims and objectives, and seems to assume that objectives are always behavioural objectives. The critics of this 'objectives philosophy' also seem to regard behavioural objectives as the only form of objectives worth discussing. Macdonald-Ross (1975), for example, seems to assume that a systematic approach to curriculum development becomes impossible without strict rules for the derivations of 'precise instructional objectives'. He labels the position of the 'softliners', i.e., those who recognize that formulation of objectives often must be based on human judgement and common sense, as 'frankly hilarious'. In my opinion, too much emphasis has been put on the *behavioural* nature of educational objectives. To the extent that teacher assessment of the success or failure of teaching is at all possible, the *criteria* for this assessment must be sought in some observable outcome that is indicative of learning, i.e., in something which results from the *behaviour* of the learner. But that does not necessarily mean that the behaviour is the *objective*. It is quite possible that the objective is a change in the learner which cannot be directly observed, except perhaps through his own introspection. The behaviour is in that case only a symptom which indicates that the objective has been achieved.

Those who insist on behavioural objectives usually solve the problem by stating objectives in terms of the 'verbal behaviour' of the learner. For example, instead of insisting that he 'understands' how an engine works, they insist that he 'explains' how it works. This can, of course, be useful as a device for reminding teachers that they must make explicit their criteria for 'understanding', 'knowing', etc. in various situations. But if we want a pupil to understand, then it is the understanding which is the objective of teaching/learning, not the explanation which demonstrates the understanding.

More important than a formulation in behavioural terms is that objectives are formulated so that they can be communicated among individuals and groups involved in the teaching-learning process. The aim must be, then, to formulate, in language which is generally understood, what the desired outcome of the teaching-learning process is. If this outcome cannot be directly observed, we need to develop means of judging whether or not the outcome is what we desired. Ultimately, our judgement will be based to a large extent on what pupils show that they can *do*, on some kind of behaviour, but it will still be judgement on the basis of empirical evidence, and not on automatic application of a 'decision algorithm'.

This distinction between the objectives of education, which may or may not be 'behavioural', and the empirical evidence on which we judge whether or not the objectives have been reached, seems to me to be particularly important in the field of reading. If reading is the *construction* or *reconstruc-*

tion of *meaning* from the printed text, then the objectives of reading instruction cannot be directly observable behaviour such as 'barking at print'. Any 'reading behaviour' which the teacher can observe is only an indication of the likelihood of ability to read. Of course, these indications are important, because it is only through a careful interpretation of them that the teacher can judge whether the various objectives of reading instruction have been achieved. But at the same time the teacher must be aware of the fact that these symptomatic behaviours do not always have a simple, straightforward relationship to the underlying ability of *deriving meaning*, the development of which is the primary objective of the teaching of reading.

Methods for developing reading skills

Even given the basic principles of teaching reading, which were quoted from Heilman earlier, various approaches to the teaching of reading in the infant school are available to the teacher. Some of them are such that to rely *solely* on them would be to violate basic principles, but all of them can be used to some extent and, when used well, should complement each other. The major approaches are:

the language-experience approach

the psycholinguistic 'guessing game' approach

the look-and-say approach

the phonics approach

Motivation of the child is the factor which should permeate the whole reading curriculum. Motivation to learn to read, and motivation to read, is both a means and an end in the reading curriculum. It is a means because the child may not participate in and benefit from all the different learning experiences organized by the teacher, unless he is motivated to do so. And motivation is an end, because one of the long-term aims of the teaching of reading is to develop in the child a lasting interest in reading and willingness to use his reading skills and to continue to develop them. The long-term aims are that the pupil should be able to cope with all the reading tasks involved in living in our society (functional literacy), and that he should be equipped to enjoy reading as a recreational activity (reading for pleasure).

The four approaches to teaching reading listed above differ considerably in the extent to which they relate to, and rely upon, the total language experience of the child. The *look-and-say* approach and the *phonics* approach involve the child largely in consideration of isolated words and linguistic units smaller than words (letters, sounds, syllables). In certain situations these approaches help to develop the child's sight vocabulary ('look-and-say') or his ability to *analyse* unknown words in order to find out how they 'sound' (phonics). The weakness of both approaches is that they do not focus upon *meaningful context* in the reading tasks. It is therefore more difficult to help children develop the ability to read whole sentences, to derive their *meaning*, if one relies solely on the 'look-and-say' and/or phonics approach to the teaching of reading.

The other two approaches, the *language-experience* approach and the *psycholinguistic 'guessing-game'* approach both rely on meaningful language as the vehicle for the teaching of reading. They can easily complement each other, since one – the language-experience approach – is essentially a method for developing suitable reading materials based on the children's own spoken language, whereas the other tries to help children to develop their comprehension skills. Through utilizing the redundancy of meaningful text, the child is encouraged to make intelligent guesses about unknown words on the basis of various context cues.

Skills hierarchies (or 'ladders')

Attempts to identify reading skills vary considerably in their emphasis and in their detail, and the very concept 'skill' does not seem to have any clear-cut, commonly accepted definition. Whether or not something is identified as a 'skill' may, to a large extent, depend on what kind of situations we observe, and what kinds of task we confront the pupils with. And whether we see something as one 'large' skill or a combination of 'smaller' skills may depend upon how we perceive the task to which the skill, or the skills, relate.

A useful method of analysing complex skills systematically is that of Gagné (1965). He defines a learning task as being composed of intellectual skills, and each single skill as being composed of subskills or component skills. Gagné treats the single skill as something given, or as something that can be immediately identified in a 'common sense' way. The strength of his model lies in the analysis of skills into subskills, and in the ordering of the subskills into a hierarchy with the single skill at the top. Gagné's model for skill analysis is based on an educational technology approach, which includes the assumption that the aims of instruction are expressed as behavioural objectives. I have already discussed (see page 47f) the view that the commonly accepted notion of behavioural objectives in a systematic approach may well be too narrowly conceived. However, the concept of skills hierarchies can, in my opinion, be very useful even if one adopts a less strictly behaviourist view of instruction than that proposed by Gagné.

Trying to build a reading curriculum through identifying important skills hierarchies which can provide the framework for the teaching provisions does not mean that the skills are seen as 'human faculties' with clear psychological or physiological correlates. Many skills are probably best understood as aspects of human ability which are singled out for practical reasons (not because they are theoretically important as constituent elements in the complex of human abilities).

Another concept that is important to the learning process is *transfer*. The most commonly recognized type of transfer is transfer *between* learning tasks. For example, learning to drive a tractor requires the mastery of some skills which prove useful in learning to drive a car. The learning of one task is said to *transfer positively* to the learning of the other. Gagné claims that there is a less common kind of transfer which relates to skill hierarchies. Within such a hierarchy, *less* complex skills transfer positively to *more* complex skills.

Reading is too complex a system of skills to lend itself to an analysis using the Gagné hierarchy model. But the levels of difficulty of printed language used for the purpose of learning to read can be fairly accurately assessed, and on this basis materials can be ordered into a hierarchical framework. Similarly, games and other educational exercises can, and should, be graded and ordered into hierarchies according to levels of difficulty. The reason for this is primarily children's needs to achieve success, and the importance of success as a motivational force in learning. Children are more likely to experience success if they encounter less difficult tasks prior to more difficult tasks, and for many pupils success will depend upon the care with which the learning experiences are graded and ordered. If a section, or appropriate group, of learning materials is graded, the resulting hierarchy or 'ladder' lends itself not only to the formulation of part of a curriculum or syllabus, but it also becomes a valuable instrument for the recording of individual pupil progress within that part of the curriculum. For outlines of typical 'ladders' of this kind, see Appendix 2.

It must be emphasized that there exists no single hierarchy or 'ladder' incorporating *all* the reading skills a child must master. The identification, definition, and ordering of skills will depend upon the method or methods of teaching which are in operation. Some methods lends themselves more readily to this kind of hierarchical ordering than others. For example, the teaching of phonics skills benefits from careful grading of the letters and letter combinations for which sounds or sound combinations have to be learned. Using other methods, separate skills or subskills are not so easy to identify, and here careful grading of the *materials* according to overall level of difficulty is the best approach to ordering.

Most infant schools make use of one, or more, of the published reading schemes (basal reading series in the USA), and these schemes are normally ordered into difficulty levels by their authors. But in this context it must be pointed out that careful grading is often achieved by an over-emphasis on vocabulary control which results in the meaningless language often described as 'primerese'.

Some benefits of hierarchy ('ladder') systems

In summary, the benefits of using a system of skills 'ladders' (hierarchies) for the language and reading curriculum are as follows:

The system

a)   ensures identification and definition of specific learning *objectives*;

b)   caters for each stage of (a) by the provision of appropriate learning *materials*;

c)   necessitates ordering of (a) and (b) into *levels of difficulty* to facilitate learning;

d)   facilitates the *monitoring* of individual pupil progress using the 'ladders' as record sheets;

e)   encourages *diagnostic teaching* in the placing of each pupil at a level which is appropriate for him;

f)   facilitates shared use of school materials and resources, and the formulation of a *school policy* in line with the recommendations of the Bullock Committee;

g)   creates a logical system through which each pupil can become actively *involved in his own progress*;

h)   enables pupils to make progress at their own *individual rates*, and the brighter children need not be held back to keep pace with others in the class;

i)   through (g) and (h), encourages in pupils, from an early age, positive attitudes to study habits of a more independent or autonomous nature.

CHAPTER 5

CURRICULUM DEVELOPMENT IN THE NURSERY AND INFANT SCHOOL

There should be positive steps to develop the language ability of children in the pre-school and nursery and infant years . . .

Every school should devise a systematic policy for the development of reading competence in pupils of all ages and ability levels.

'A Language for Life'
(HMSO 1975)

Some philosophical implications

A search among the many published volumes about early education reveals the curious fact that there is rarely any philosophical discussion of the *aims* and *objectives* of nursery or infant teaching. Most writers seem to assume that there is widespread tacit understanding of what should go on in nursery or infant classrooms – an intuitive consensus of opinion which can be taken as read. The assumption seems to be that we all know what these authors mean when they are making vague statements. This attitude is exemplified in the Plowden Report (DES 1967), where we read about the 'better infant schools' and the 'best infant schools' without any indication of the criteria by which these judgements are made. The 'needs' of young children are frequently referred to, without any attempt at a definition of them.

Dearden (1972) points out that the concept of 'need' is being more and more widely used in discussions about curriculum design. In the DES report 'Primary Education' (DES 1959) it is stated that

> one salient feature of primary education today is the ever deepening concern with children as children.

This is elaborated upon as follows:

> This concern shows itself especially in the awareness of the child as a whole with inter-dependent spiritual, emotional, intellectual and physical *needs*.

Of a similar report on primary education in Scotland, Dearden (1972) writes:

> The first chapter is devoted, not to a discussion of relevant aims of education, but to the 'needs' of the child, which turn out to be just five in number.

And the most recent report of this kind, 'Primary Education in England' (DES 1978), states:

> Primary schools have to provide for children with a variety of different needs
> . . .

There must obviously be some degree of value judgement and personal opinion regarding what these 'needs' really are and how they should be catered for in the primary school. But, as Dearden emphasizes, if we centre curriculum discussion on a concept like 'need', we should at least expect each user of the term to provide his or her definition of it. And any definition of 'need' must make it clear that to identify an educational 'need' is to make some kind of subjective value judgement – except perhaps in the case of the most basic needs for food, shelter, etc., which can be said to be objectively observable. Since the 'needs' which the school is supposed to cater for are typically ill defined, it must be the duty of every educationist to examine each 'need' critically, and try to determine how – if at all – the 'need' can be translated into practical educational objectives for the teacher.

'Growth' is another favourite concept in books about infant education. This concept is even more deceptively simple than 'need', because of the association with biological growth where everything is 'taken care of' by nature. Exactly what is meant by 'growth' does not become any clearer when we are exhorted to 'foster growth' in a variety of areas related to personality, creativity, etc. Once again the cosy conspiracy prevails. 'We all *know* how to foster all kinds of growth in young human beings' is the sentiment implicit in so many of the books on early schooling. This is a dangerous sentiment, mainly because it encourages us to support the 'cosy conspiracy', and discourages the asking of important questions. But there are many questions which a teacher *should* ask, as soon as he is advised to foster a certain kind of 'growth' in her pupils. For example:

a) What exactly is meant by this kind of 'growth'?

b) What kind of result of end product should the 'growth' lead to?

c) Who says that this 'growth' is a desirable aim?

d) What evidence is there that it is desirable?

e) What evidence is there that I can foster it?

f) How can I go about fostering this 'growth'?

g) How can I monitor my pupils' progress in this 'growth' process?

These are the kinds of questions teachers should ask, if they want to go beyond the stage of what Dearden calls 'high-sounding platitudes'.

Theories concerning the education of children are bedevilled by facile analogies. An example of this is found in Holt (1964). Discussing the curriculum, Holt writes:

> 'School should be a great *smörgasbord* of intellectual, artistic, creative and athletic activities, from which each child could take whatever he wanted, and as much as he wanted, or as little.'

At a glance this appears to be the whole, simple solution to our curriculum problems but, as soon as one begins to examine the implications, it appears not only impractical, but undesirable as a curriculum concept. It is only through education that a pupil can develop the ability to benefit from such a wealth of choice. Some children are sufficiently privileged to receive this kind of education within their families, through being introduced to a range of worthwhile leisure activities and thus being helped to develop their own interests and tastes. But many children are not privileged in this respect. They need help from their teachers in order to develop their interests, tastes, and judgements. So in addition to being impractical, the 'smörgasbord' philosophy as a basis for the primary school curriculum does not mean that the pupils should not be offered *any* choice in their work or play activities. On the contrary, there should be periods of the school day, at every stage of schooling, when the children are free to choose from a wide range of activities. So the 'smörgasbord' has its place in the school menu, but only as part of a carefully balanced diet.

Dearden (1972) discusses the ideas of Dewey in the context of 'growth' theory, and makes the following point:

> Dewey set aside all biological and horticultural analogies for a conception of education as an essentially *social process* and one in which our *experiences* and *understanding* are *constantly reconstructed and reorganized*. What is underestimated and understressed in Dewey, however, is the extent to which the teacher must be an *active interventionist* and *leader* in this process, often having positively to explain, instruct and insist, as well as to guide and stimulate. (my italics)

It is this view of the importance of the teacher's active role in infant education which underpins my work in the field of curriculum development. A key concept in this context is that education is a *social process*. There is a wealth of evidence within the field of child development to the effect that the socialization process of the child is closely linked to the development of language and thought (see e.g., Gahagan and Gahagan 1970, Halliday 1973, Labov 1970, Lawton 1968, Tough 1974 and 1976). Children's language and thought processes become manifest in the four communication skill areas: listening, speaking, reading, and writing. *The fostering and development of these communication skills must therefore be central to an infant school curriculum.*

Two kinds of play

Another key concept in infant education is *play*, which is of great importance for healthy child development. But here again the teacher should tread warily and avoid a facile acceptance of the concept of any kind of play as, without qualifications and in all circumstances, a valuable and desirable occupation for young children of infant school age. Parry and Archer (1975) point out that play can be used in two ways: 'One merely keeps children occupied; the other contributes to their educational development.'

Unfortunately, infant school curriculum planning does not become a *fait accompli* simply by the setting up of certain play situations in the classroom. The play situations are means to an end, not an end in themselves.

If there is no scope for development within the play activity, development cannot take place. A high degree of teacher professionalism is required in order to monitor individual pupil progress by means of a stimulating range of play activities. The infant school curriculum should provide for *well-planned* and *guided* play with adequate, skilled adult intervention; play which specifically aims at developing in the child language skills, mathematical skills, and scientific concepts. These should lead him into the realms of investigation, exploration, and problem solving. A valuable source book and guide in the field of educational play is *Structuring Play in the Early Years at School* (Manning and Sharp 1977), which reports a large-scale Schools Council project on play in the infant school. In outlining ways in which their book may be used by teachers in infant schools, the authors use italics to make the point that

> [the book] does not suggest that children will 'pick up' the skills of reading and writing, nor that numeracy is acquired by chance in their play. These skills need to be taught by a teacher.

Teaching basic skills through play (the teacher's role)

Play, in a loose, unstructured sense, is not the panacea of infant education. It is only when it is skilfully planned and structured that it becomes a very wonderful, dynamic central force in the education of young children. An exception must be made, however, in the case of imaginative or fantasy play, which almost invariably stimulates and absorbs infant school children. Acting out stories, 'let's pretend' or 'dressing up' games require little intervention from the teacher, although here, too, the introduction of some new vocabulary will usually enhance the learning potential of the game. Many kinds of learning may be taking place, as the children pretend to be nurses, doctors, grocers, spacemen, hairdressers, etc., and clearly this kind of play cannot be structured or systematized.

It is in the field of basic skills learning that the need for system and structure becomes important. Here the range and scope of play activities cannot be left to the imagination of the children, in the hope that they will make progress by 'accident' or by 'discovery'. Play materials and equipment must be incorporated into a carefully planned curriculum of learning, and the teacher must guide pupils, in groups or, when necessary, individually, through this curriculum. Here professional work in this context includes:

1 *Defining* objectives
2. *Identifying* useful materials and/or play equipment
3 *Grading* these into levels of difficulty
4 *Structuring* the play activities accordingly

5 *Evaluating* individual pupil progress *and* the effectiveness of the mals/equipment

6 *Recording* individual pupil progress

7 *Involving* each pupil as an active agent in his own progress

A systematic approach to language and reading

Compared with most other subject areas in our schools, language and reading are relatively neglected fields of curriculum development. They are different from traditional subject areas in that they are concerned with basic communication skills which are utilized in almost every area of learning. This is clearly reflected in the volume of readings entitled *The Reading Curriculum* (Melnik and Merritt 1972), which to a great extent deals with questions about the place of reading in the curriculum, rather than with the curriculum of reading. *The Reading Curriculum* is, in the words of its editors, based on the following assumptions:

1. Reading is a tangible manifestation of talking, learning and thinking. Therefore, continuous development of reading can result in improved talking, learning and thinking.

2. Reading unifies the related language arts of writing, listening and speaking. . . . Therefore, reading integrates and affects the nature and quality of oral and written language.

3. *Reading permeates the curriculum and is a major source of knowledge in every subject field*. Therefore, instruction in reading should be an integral part of every reading experience in every subject. (*op. cit.*, my italics)

Reading cannot be separated from the other areas of language skills: speaking, listening, and writing. Consequently, not only reading, but the whole field of language and reading permeates the school curriculum. This means that the curriculum of language and reading becomes difficult to define in terms of its content. In this respect the language and reading curriculum is very different from, for example, the science curriculum, where it is possible to describe in some detail a satisfactory curriculum. In the field of language and reading the curriculum must instead be defined mainly in terms of the skills which the pupils are expected to acquire.

For the infant school, the language and reading curriculum is more easily defined than for the junior and secondary schools, since it consists primarily of laying the foundations for that development of basic skills which is expected to continue throughout the school years. As far as reading is concerned, the infant school curriculum is, in other words, mainly focused on the process of *learning to read*, whereas during later school years the emphasis is primarily on *reading to learn*. But there is, of course, a great deal of overlap between the stages. The process of learning to read does not end with the acquisition of basic reading skills in the infant school. Higher-order reading skills need to be developed both at junior and at secondary levels. And the first experiences of reading to learn should certainly happen during the infant school years.

Learning to read, in its widest sense, is a long-term developmental process. Reading is, as has already been pointed out, one of the four major language communication skills:

listening

speaking

reading

writing

These four areas of language skills should be seen as interdependent. It can therefore be argued that the development of reading skills begins in infancy, as the young child listens and speaks, and the whole complex of communication skills starts to grow as if by compound interest. This process of development then goes on throughout childhood and adolescence, into adulthood, and throughout life, although the degree of later development is likely to vary considerably depending upon the needs and interests of the adult.

The fact that reading development is intimately related to language development does not mean, however, that this development comes 'naturally' like children's physical development. The development of most language and reading skills needs to be stimulated in a systematic and organized way, something which is possible only if one has a fairly clear idea about which are the most important skills, and how and in what order these skills can be developed.

Language and reading can be conceived as a complex of closely interrelated skills and subskills, which form a 'semi-hierarchical' order, i.e., there exists hierarchy within the complex, with skills ranging from lower-order to higher-order skills, but all the skills and subskills cannot be ordered into one single hierarchy. This means that some skills may develop in parallel, or simultaneously, while other skills develop in a serial fashion, so that the second skills build on the first, the third build on the second, and so on.

We are, then, dealing with a continuously developing, highly complex system of skills. Any reading curriculum must take this aspect of reading into account, and this can, in the opinion of many reading experts, best be achieved through a systematic, structured approach to the teaching of reading, or, more precisely, to the *organization of provisions for learning to read*. A systematic approach presupposes a theoretical basis or framework which can guide the curriculum development. Such a framework can be provided by *educational technology*.

How can educational technology assist curriculum development?

There is a fairly common misconception about educational technology, according to which it is defined narrowly as dealing with 'learning by machines or other audio-visual aids'. In fact, the word 'technology means *control*, and so educational technology is an approach to teaching/learning which emphasizes the need for control of the educational process and of the outcomes of that process.

Educational technology can be defined as

the *development,*
    application,
    evaluation   of *systems,*
                        techniques,
                        aids

for the purpose of *improving the process of human learning*

It follows from this definition that the use of aids in the form of machines and/or other audio-visual equipment *may* be included in the systematic attempt to promote learning. But these machines or this equipment will then be *part* of the system, and by no means the sum total of it. And many systems developed through an educational technology approach may do without any kind of machinery or sophisticated audio-visual equipment.

Rowntree (1974) describes educational technology as follows:

> it is concerned with the design and evaluation of curricula and learning experiences and with the problems of implementing and renovating them.

Essentially, it is a rational, problem-solving approach to education, a way of *thinking* sceptically and systematically about education.

The hallmark of educational technology is a *systematic approach* to problems of teaching and learning, and an emphasis on *evaluation* as an intrinsic part of the educational process. The emphasis on evaluation is, to use Rowntree's words, a result of 'thinking sceptically' about education. A healthy scepticism does not mean that one denies the possibility that a particular approach to teaching or learning can be effective. It simply means that one does not take the effect for granted, but recognizes the need to find some *evidence* of the effect.

Both the systematic approach and the emphasis on evaluation seem particularly valuable in the field of reading and language development. The systematic approach should make it easier to ensure that all relevant aspects of the highly complex sets of skills are covered, and evaluation is important in order to guide the teacher in his or her choice of materials and methods used to help the child to learn to read. Evaluation is also crucial when it comes to deciding when a particular stage in the learning process is completed and the child is ready for the next stage.

The important features of curriculum development through educational technology may be summarized as follows:

1 the focus of attention is on techniques for *learning* rather than for teaching, and the apporach is therefore *pupil centred*

2 '*systems*' and *techniques* imply a variety of approaches to the learning of any skill, thus catering for individual pupil preferences and differences

3 *evaluation* is central, and implies continuous monitoring
   (a) of individual pupil progress, and
   (b) of all components used in the learning process.

An educational technology apporach is, of necessity, based on the assumption that the methods and materials to be used to promote learning cannot be prescribed *once and for all* on the basis of *a priori* knowledge of the 'right' way to teach reading. Instead the teaching of reading should be organized in the best possible way given present resources, knowledge, and experience, and keeping an open mind vis-à-vis any possibilities of improvement in the light of new knowledge and experience or new resources.

Models for curriculum planning and development in an educational technology framework have been suggested by a number of authors (see e.g., Briggs 1968, Davies and Hartley 1972, Popham and Baker 1970, and Wheeler 1967). Most models describe a cyclic process starting with certain aims, goals, and objectives and ending with some kind of evaluation, which provides the basis for a decision about whether or not the goals have been achieved. Since it is not always the case that the goals have been achieved after the first cycle, the outcome of the first cycle usually provides the starting point for the second cycle, and so on. The aims, goals, and objectives may or may not be revised after each cycle, depending on whether they seem realistic in view of previous results.

It is useful to differentiate between long-term aims and objectives, on the one hand, and short-term objectives, on the other. The long-term aims can be expected to be unchanged over a long period, although we must always be open to the need for changes in the light of evaluation results, or as a response to new ideas about what the aims of education should be. The short-term objectives are selected with reference *both* to the long-term aims and to the results of previous evaluation. This means, of course, that even the first cycle from objectives to evaluation should be preceded by some kind of evaluation. Such initial evaluation is usually called *diagnosis*. The short-term objectives have to be determined anew for each cycle in the process. There are three alternatives:

1   keeping the short-term objectives unchanged, which implies that one has to try to find a new way of achieving them;

2   selecting new short-term objectives, which implies that the previous set of objectives has been achieved;

3   revising the short-term objectives, which implies that the existing ones are not likely to be achieved.

A schematic illustration of a typical curriculum planning and implementation cycle based on an educational technology approach is shown in Figure 2. The evaluation stage, which is the last in each cycle, is of key importance, because the result of the evaluation determines whether the pupil proceeds towards a new set of objectives, whether he must continue in his attempts to achieve the original set of objectives, or whether the original objectives must be revised. If the pupil has to continue to attempt to achieve the original objectives (or a revised version of them), the evaluation result must also contribute to the selection of a new set of materials and methods, which might more successfully help the pupil to achieve the objectives.

Evaluation has, then, the dual function of providing guidelines for the pupil's progress towards a given set of objectives, and of providing a basis for revision of the initial objectives, in order to adapt them better to the learning potential of the pupil. In this way evaluation becomes evaluation both of the pupil's progress, and of the suitability of the learning process and its objectives. But it is *not* evaluation of the pupil for the sake of classifying or labelling him.

It must be noted that there is often no strictly objective way of determining whether a given evaluation result should be seen as evidence of the pupil's need of further learning, or of the need to revise the initial objective. In other words, it must often be left to the judgement of teacher and/or learner to decide whether failure to reach a goal means that the way to reach it was not well chosen, or that the goal itself was not suitable for that learner at that time. This has been seen as a fundamental weakness of this kind of goal-directed systematic approach (see e.g., Macdonald-Ross 1975). It would indeed be a serious weakness if this approach were expected to constitute a process for *automatic* and *strictly rule-governed* solution of teaching/learning problems in a self-contained system. There is, however, no need to see educational technology and the systematic approach to learning in such a way. It can, and, in my opinion, should, be seen rather as a method of systematizing our attempts to organize teaching and learning in the best

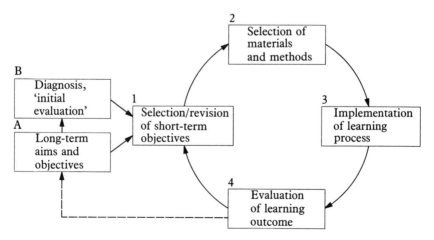

Figure 2   Schematic illustration of a curriculum planning and implementation cycle.

possible way, and of continuously trying to improve this organization (a very similar view is expressed by Rowntree, 1974). According to this view, educational technology does not provide – or even try to provide – a means of making human judgement superfluous in the development and implementation of a curriculum; it 'only' provides a means of ensuring that human judgement is guided as far as possible by empirical evidence obtained in a *systematic* rather than a *random* way.

CHAPTER 6

A SYSTEMATIC LANGUAGE AND READING CURRICULUM

We advocate, in short, planned intervention in the child's language development . . .

'A Language for Life'
(HMSO 1975)

Language development through play

Gahagan and Gahagan (1970) reported the development of an innovatory curriculum for the improvement of spoken language, devised by the authors and implemented and evaluated in nine infant schools in London. Their stated aim was

> to produce a programme which any teacher with a standard training could use in the ordinary classroom. We aimed to teach children to use a language both formal and flexible – the one through which education is mediated – the only one in which expression can fit individual experience and needs.

The Gahagan programme was based on a set of eleven language games which are described in their report. These games were shown to be successful in furthering the children's language development, and, in particular, their programme seemed beneficial for children at the lower ability levels and for immigrant children.

When I decided to try to test my ideas empirically through the development and implementation of an experimental curriculum, it became clear to me that language games should play an important part in that curriculum. The games to be used in the experimental curriculum were derived from two sources. Firstly, some of the games described by Gahagan and Gahagan (1970, Chapter 4) were adopted, while others were slightly adapted. Secondly, a number of language games devised, field-tested, and revised by a group of ILEA infant teachers and headteachers were used. The latter set of games was developed at the ILEA Centre for Urban Educational Studies (CUES) and published by the ILEA Learning Materials Service.

All of these language games, both the Gahagan games and the CUES games, are designed to involve small groups of infant school children (normally five – seven years old) in play situations where language is most likely to be generated in the process of purposeful communication. Language is *required* of the players as an integrated part of the game.

During the first meetings of the CUES workshop group, under the direction of Jim Wight, a great deal of discussion centred around the fundamental purpose of games of this kind. This involved questions of the kind which all teachers, and perhaps especially teachers of young children, ought to be asking continuously, namely:

What activities are going on in my classroom today?

What is the educational rationale for them?

What are my educational objectives?

Can the objectives be reconciled with the long-term aims of education?

Are my pupils benefiting from what they are doing?

How can I find out if they are benefiting?

These questions imply a kind of accountability to oneself which demands a high degree of professional rigour and energy, perhaps too high a degree if the teacher is working in isolation and not as part of a team of active professional colleagues. But it is a major responsibility of heads of schools to direct and support the entire staff in this process of curriculum evaluation and reappraisal. Adequate time must be allocated for staff discussion. This is what a school 'policy' is all about.

A central question in the development of the CUES games concerned the *nature* of the language which they should elicit and promote. After all, children communicate among themselves frequently in the normal course of play. What *special, educationally valuable* features should these language games help to develop in the young children? The answer to this question was a list of educational objectives which are almost identical to those published in Chapter 5 of the Bullock Report (DES 1975), the chapter entitled 'Language in the early years':

> planned intervention . . . will mean that the teacher recognises the need for the child to include in his experience the following uses of language, and that she will then keep an effective record of his progress in them:
>
> 1 Reporting on present and recalled experiences
>
> 2 Collaborating towards agreed ends
>
> 3 Projecting into the future: anticipating and predicting
>
> 4 Projecting and comparing possible alternatives
>
> 5 Perceiving causal and dependent relationships
>
> 6 Giving explanations of how and why things happen
>
> 7 Expressing and recognising tentativeness
>
> 8 Dealing with problems in the imagination and seeing possible solutions
>
> 9 Creating experiences through the use of imagination
>
> 10 Justifying behaviour
>
> 11 Reflecting on feelings, own and other people's.

These objectives cannot be treated separately, and none of them can be fully achieved through the playing of one single language game. It is unrealistic to demand specific results in terms of any *one* of the objectives from the playing of one particular game. What is achieved is practice and experience in using the forms of language engendered by the nature of the game. Some of the games tend to generate precise, accurate descriptive language, while others elicit language which is more imaginative and creative. But *all* the games serve to achieve certain educationally valuable aims, for example:

1   good social behaviour and cooperative attitudes in group activities

2   some degree of independence through working in groups with only *partial* teacher supervision (after the game has been taught by the teacher)

3   the development of listening skills

4   thoughtful response to the ideas of other pupils

5   clarity of meaning and expression in spoken language

6   extension of vocabulary and of forms of language usage (phrases and sentences)

If the language generated by any individual game is analysed, it will be found that certain of the Bullock Report objectives quoted earlier are involved to a high degree.

In all cases, it is important to point out that each game has to be taught by the teacher before children can be expected to play with only intermittent teacher supervision. Teaching the game, or introducing a new version or level of the game, is the time for the teacher's contribution to the extension of the pupils' vocabulary. New vocabulary should be introduced and given real meaning in terms of the pupils' understanding. The new language is then used and practised in the course of the language game.

Description of the language games

The language games used in my experimental language and reading curriculum are described below.

Story sequencing games

Sets of picture cards, containing from three to six pictures per set, were used for groups of children to arrange in sequence and then describe the events depicted in the form of a story. The sequence is often variable, so that each child has to make a choice of sequence, and is then required to justify his preference – by telling the others why he has put them in that order. Some of the stories are dramatic, some are funny, and most are open-ended, giving scope for the imagination of the child.

The children play this game in groups of three or four, taking it in turns to put the pictures in their preferred order, listening to any criticism of that order from the other players, responding, and answering questions. Essentially, the exercise entails logical thinking, listening, and the ability to explain, describe, and justify situations and decisions relating to the pictures. Imagination is involved as the story may develop beyond the scenes depicted.

The most successful sets of pictures are those which relate to the interests of the pupils and involve the children emotionally or imaginatively. A cassette or tape recorder may be used to record each child's story after discussion has led to his 'final version'. If any of the children are later doing some free writing based on the stories, the tape can be rewound by individual pupils who want to remind themselves of words used by themselves or by other pupils.

Ask and find out

Each game in this set is a large board game, and the children playing are required to develop skills of enquiry. The players ask each other questions in order to find out precisely where a hidden treasure is, or an animal, or some other thing. A particular strategy is required in each game, and the techniques of enquiry are developed throughout the sequence of the games.

Language skills developed through these games include listening, naming, describing, and categorizing. The demands of the game are such that the children's vocabulary is invariably extended. The game can be played by a group of two, three, or four children.

Route games

This is a series of board games designed to encourage children to develop the skills of differentiating, describing, and questioning. Pupils may play the games in pairs or in small groups. One child (or a pair of children working together) holds the route card which shows the 'right' route through a magic wood, into a besieged castle, etc. The other children have to ask questions that can be answered with 'Yes' or 'No', in order to find the route that leads to the goal.

In each case the options to be described require careful differentiation which necessitates careful language. In these route games children become involved in the drama of the story which underpins the game. If the central character in the story is to make progress, precise and detailed description is essential in order to identify various features along the route. It is interesting to hear the children building on each other's growing vocabulary as the game progresses. Different routes are possible by permutation of the options at each stage, and so there are several different route cards for each game.

Collecting Sets (a version of 'Happy Families')

These games use packs of picture cards and are played in small groups. Each player has to describe, or ask questions about, the pictures on the cards in order to win them. As they play, the children discover which attributes of the illustrations depicted they need to describe with precision to make their communication effective. Gradually they increase their skill in selecting and formulating language appropriate to the task, and to the knowledge and understanding of other players.

The sets of pictures are structured so that they become increasingly demanding in terms of observation and description of detail as the players become more and more sophisticated in their language usage.

Listen, Discuss, and Do

The games in this category involve a group of three or four children in discussions about which option to choose from a series of alternatives. The task can, for example, consist of designing a creature from outer space, using a workbook or a kit containing alternative 'creature parts', such as limbs, eyes, means of transport, etc. A tape recording is prepared for each game, and one child is given the job of 'controller and chairman'. The children listen to the instructions on the tape/cassette which direct their attention to the available options and tell them what function a given part should have. The children then talk about the various alternatives, their advantages and disadvantages, and try to agree on one single alternative as the best option.

This kind of game is very valuable for encouraging children to express tentative opinions (perhaps, don't you think ? what about ? . . .), to formulate hypotheses, and to give and respond to constructive criticism.

I Am the Teacher

This kind of game is played by two players, who sit at desks facing each other, but concealed from each other by a screen. Both children have a set of small toys or other objects and a board on which to arrange them. The two sets of toys or objects and the two boards are identical. The child who is 'teacher' arranges his toys/objects one by one on his board, while giving the other player precise instructions so that the 'pupil' can put his toys/objects in exactly the same way. Farm animals can be used, in which case the board is a plan of the farm. Or the board can show a street map, where model cars are to be placed. The game can also be played with pieces of felt in different colours and shapes, which can be placed in patterns directly on the desks. There are, of course, many other possibilities, depending on the availability of materials and the imagination of the teacher.

Surprise Box

This is a version of what is often called 'Kim's Game'. A number of small objects are used, the number being increased as the players become more experienced. A set of objects might comprise, for example, a match, a matchbox, a toothpick, a pencil, a ruler, a candle, a nail file. One player chooses an object and describes it aloud to the other players – its shape, number of sides, relative size, nature of surface, etc. When a player thinks he can tell which object is being described, he raises his hand. If he is correct, it is his turn to describe an object.

When the pupils are sufficiently practised, the objects are all put into a tall box, and one player must put his hand into the box, select an object, identify it by touch and describe it, while the others listen to the description and try to identify it, using their memory of the objects that are in the box.

The importance of teacher involvement

In all respects these games have shown themselves to be as enjoyable as, and often more enjoyable than, the more common 'Snakes and Ladders' and 'Ludo'. These games are much varied, more demanding, more education-ally valuable than the usual Christmas gift assortment.

In order that these games achieve their full educational potential, the teacher must be aware of her role in the learning process.

a) The teacher must *teach* the game to each group (while other group activities engage the rest of the class). With most children the teacher must provide a *'language input'*, an introduction of key words and concepts, explaining carefully the importance of these words. Without this 'language input', the 'language output' generated among the children playing the games will be limited.

b) The teacher must not expect any group to play profitably for any great length of time without her supervision. As she circulates among the children engaged in other kinds of activities, like painting, writing, reading, weighing, modelling, she must return regularly to the language game groups to encourage and elicit responses.

c) The teacher needs to select the group carefully to achieve the most beneficial interaction among the children. A confident rather overbearing child should not play with three timid, much less articulate children. The little 'boss' should ideally be balanced by at least one other child who is confident and articulate.

d) Individual pupil progress requires to be recorded, and the teacher will have to observe and participate in the games to find out if each pupil is making progress towards the next higher level. It is also important to ensure that all children have experience of all kinds of games in a structured progression.

Video-recordings have been made which show groups of children playing the language games instructed and supervised by teachers. These videotapes together with notes are available from Drake Educational Associates Ltd., 212 Whitechurch Road, Cardiff, CF4 3XF.

Structuring language games and reading materials

The games described in the previous section are easily organized into levels of difficulty on the basis of their degree of complexity. For example, in Story Sequencing, the games involving only three cards for sorting provide a simpler level than those involving four cards. In 'Listen, Discuss, and Do', the demands of the series of games begin at a very simple level and gradually increase until quite sophisticated language is being used and generated.

In order that the structure of the games series is made clear, and to facilitate storage and retrieval of the games as well as recordkeeping of pupil progress, it is useful to type the names of all the games in a series onto a 'ladder' of the kind discussed earlier (Chapter 4). The games are entered in *ascending* order of difficulty, starting at the bottom 'rung' with the easiest game. The record will then show the child 'climbing up the ladder' as he progresses through the series of games.

The skills 'ladder' can then be extended into a matrix by means of adding columns for information about teacher introduction, amont of practice playing the game, etc. If copies of this matrix are reproduced for each pupil, it is a simple matter to keep these copies in a ring binder and to monitor individual pupil progress throughout the series of games, which constitutes a vital part of the systematically organized language and reading curriculum (see pages 67-72).

The 'ladder-matrices' used in the experimental curriculum, the evaluation of which is described later in this book (Chapter 8) are reproduced in Appendix 1. For a more detailed discussion of the systematic ordering of skills and materials to promote the development of these skills, see Hunter (1977). The actual form, contents, and column headings for each 'ladder-matrix' are details which each team of teachers must discuss in order to meet the requirements of their own pupils and utilize the resources available to them. Each set of matrices should be revised and amended regularly, as new materials are added to the resources of the school.

It must be emphasized that although the Gagné model was a starting point and inspiration for the ladder and matrix format of work schemes and record sheets used in this approach to curriculum development, this does not mean that Gagné learning theory is an ideal model for the learning of the complex skills involved in language and literacy, e.g., of comprehension. The theory provides a good framework which facilitates the structuring of books, games, and other materials into levels of difficulty. This is the feature of Gagné's model which has been primarily capitalized upon here.

Once sorting and ordering of all the materials are done, and the various 'ladder work sheets' are duplicated, a structured approach to the curriculum is relatively easy to manage. The pupils are much more likely to experience success within a planned and carefully graded framework, and the inclusion of a variety of enjoyable games and story books makes it easy to avoid the kind of rigid, formal, or too predictable routine which sometimes is associated with carefully planned and ordered classroom work. The system also allows flexibility, since children can easily move 'sideways' from a certain level of one activity 'ladder' to a similar level on another 'ladder'. And they can miss out entire steps on a 'ladder' if their progress warrants this.

If the graded series of resources (reading books, story books, games, etc.) is extensive, and provides for a wide range of ability, no pupil in any class should be prevented from making progress at his optimum rate. The system makes individualized instruction a practical reality.

Published reading schemes

Reading schemes which use contrived and unnatural language prevent children from developing the ability to detect sequential probability in linguistic structure.

'A Language for Life'
(HMSO 1975)

Published reading schemes (basal reading series in the USA) are normally organized into levels of difficulty by the authors and editors. Each scheme is accompanied by a teacher's manual, and it is important that teachers using the scheme should have a copy of the manual for continuous reference. Together with notes relating to the theory underpinning the series, the manual contains guidance about the best use of supplementary materials, where these are available.

Because of the structured form of published reading schemes, it is relatively simple to incorporate them into series of graded materials (which, as we have seen, can become individual pupil record sheets). While it is true to say that all reading materials used in a school should be offered to pupils in a suitably graded order of difficulty, care should be taken in *equating* levels from a variety of reading schemes.

Many schemes have as one of their main features strict vocabulary control, and the required vocabulary may be quite different from one scheme to another. Level 2 of a given scheme, for example, always presupposes that the child has acquired the vocabulary of level 1 *of that scheme*. To go from level 2 of one scheme (where the child has mastered level 1) to level 2 of another scheme (without having mastered its level 1) does, therefore, not mean moving 'sideways' within the same level of difficulty. It usually means facing new difficulties, particularly if the language used in the scheme is such that the unfamiliar words cannot be understood from context.

If books from several reading schemes are to be used in the systematized language and reading curriculum, the teacher must examine each scheme carefully and assess its strengths and weaknesses, and determine how the different schemes relate to each other in terms of vocabulary, language, assumptions about the nature of the reading process, etc. The possible effect on children's motivation to read must also be taken into account. In this assessment of reading schemes the teacher must keep in mind constantly the long-term aims of reading instruction. It should not be taken for granted that 'any reading task is as good as another', or that any material that has been published is suitable for any group of beginning readers.

The first books with which a child is confronted are usually colourful picture books, and these tend to have a strong appeal. But will a child's first *reading* book have a strong appeal? Common sense suggests that the first reading books should be as appealing, exciting, and stimulating as possible. Will the dialogue, the 'story line', prove to be sufficiently motivating to make the beginning reader persevere with the difficult task of making sense of the strange hieroglyphics 'between' the pictures? A survey of early books in most published reading schemes yields surprisingly negative evidence in this respect.

It is worth taking some care and time to convince children that the stories are, in fact, conveyed by the print. This is not as obvious to some children as we tend to believe. Reid (1966) has shown that young children are not always aware that an adult is *reading* a story from a book rather than telling it, while looking at the pictures. And we are inclined to use terms like 'sound', 'word', and 'letter' before children understand what these terms signify. While reading a story of Cinderella to a class of infants, the teacher is inclined to turn her book towards the children to point out the illustrations. It would be more valuable to point out a bit of the text to the children and say, for example:

> 'Look, this is the part that tells me what the prince said . . . Here's Cinderella's name . . . Look! . . . Can you see it anywhere else on the page?'

This kind of exercise is more easily done with a small group than with a whole class.

The language-experience approach helps children to appreciate the fact that 'writing' or 'print' conveys *meaning*. The first awareness of this should have provided a very personal experience for the child, because his very own thoughts were noted and then read to him. It is important that his first reading book relate to these rich, personal reading experiences, but in many cases a child's first school reading book is sadly devoid of interest for him, and often devoid of meaning too. A little boy of 5½ was asked what he was reading, and he replied, 'My reading book.' When asked what it was about, he looked puzzled, and then explained, 'It's *not* about *anything* – it's my *reading* book!'

For many, many children coping with commonly used reading schemes, this is a perfectly valid comment. In the attempt to control and repeat vocabulary, or to increase the frequency of certain 'sounds', some very strange prose has come into being, and has been accepted by teachers over the years. And, regrettably, some recently published schemes also feature this unnatural language which is sometimes called 'primerese' (because it is found nowhere but in 'primers').

Nonmotivating 'primerese' nonsense

The recognition that reading is getting meaning from print implies that there is meaning in the print, and it underlines the importance of a wide range of supportive cues in the reading process. Words in themselves have often very little meaning, but when words are put together into sentences they take on meaning from each other, so that the meaning of the sentence is something more than the sum of 'meanings' of individual words. And when sentences are put together into a meaningful and interesting story, each sentence takes on a more specific and clear meaning *as part of the story*. In this way a meaningful *context* is created, and this context provides cues that are crucial to the reader.

The need for cues by which children are helped to *predict*, to make an intelligent guess about an unknown word, a guess which can then be verified or corrected, this need makes a nonsense of the kind of text that relies on excessive repetition of words and phrases without foundation in any 'story line'. Take, for example, the following passages:

No, no, Tip.

No, no.

Here, Tip,

here is Peter

Peter, Peter

Peter is here.

No, no, Tip.

Come John, come. Look John, look.

Come John, come and look.

See the ships. Look John, see the

ships. John, John, see the ships.

Come and look, see the ships.

A survey by Goodacre (1967) esablished that the scheme from which the second quotation is taken was used in *81 percent* of the infant schools surveyed, although not necessarily as the only reading scheme. A 1978 survey by Grundin (forthcoming), including 631 British infant schools, enquired more specifically about schemes in *regular* use as part of the reading curriculum, and he found that 33 percent of the schools still use that scheme regularly.

Reading matter of this kind is not likely to motivate the child towards the task of reading, nor is he likely to be able to use any powers of prediction to help him through the passage. Discussing some of the reading schemes which feature repetition at the expense of meaning and interest, Peters (1971) writes: 'As vehicles of meaning they were a complete failure; as stimulants to literacy, they were disastrous.' The use of the past tense here is, unfortunately, inappropriate, as schemes of this kind are still very widely used.

What little 'story line' there is in most reading scheme passages is often obscured rather than highlighted by the illustrations. The function of illustrations should be to provide additional context, over and above the context of previous and following sentences. But far too often illustrations do not serve this function. For example, in one widely used reading scheme, there is an illustration which shows three boys running, one of them holding a big yellow kite. Their dog is standing on its hind legs, and at the foot of the picture there is a tiny red ball. The young reader's attention will almost certainly focus on the kite, which might even be an unfamiliar object to him. The text, however, refers to the ball. And the speaker is not, as one might think, one of the boys, but the dog who wants to play with the ball. This difficulty to identify the speaker by means of the illustrations characterizes many reading scheme passages.

In her study of the reading schemes used in infant schools, Goodacre (1967) found that most schools used more than one scheme, but the schemes could be described as similar in approach, based on the principles of vocabulary control and strict limitations of the number of words used in each book, i.e., the principles that lead to 'primerese'. Vocabulary control is, in my opinion, a legitimate criterion, but only in conjunction with other, more important criteria, such as meaning and relevance to the interests and experience of the child.

Many of the commonly used reading schemes are written in the same kind of 'primerese' as the two examples given earlier. Grundin's 1978 survey gives evidence that this kind of reading scheme written in 'primerese' is used regularly in 85 percent of our infant schools. And 74 percent of the schools are using one of the ten most common 'primerese' schemes as their principal reading scheme.

When publishers are questioned about their unwillingness to abandon or revise 'primerese' schemes, they can usually quote sales figures which indicate that these schemes are still in demand. It would appear that headteachers and teachers have become immune to the nonsensical language, and are satisfied that their pupils learn to read through these schemes. This may be true of the majority of pupils, but a substantial minority of children are not successful in their attempts to learn to read. And it cannot be assumed that those who do learn through 'primerese' would not learn to read with greater facility and enthusiasm using reading books which make sense. Considering the long-term aims of the teaching of reading, it may well be that early exposure to more meaningful texts would result in fewer 'ex-literate' children, that is, children who have learned to read but who have no interest in reading.

Headteachers may claim that they cannot afford the investment necessary to abandon one reading scheme and replace it with a better one. It must be realized, though, that this is mainly a question of priorities in using the resources available to each school. I can think of no more beneficial way of spending educational monies than by a thorough reappraisal and overhaul of the reading materials in use, especially the reading schemes.

The reading books must motivate beginning readers to make the effort to find out 'what they are about'. Children should be rewarded for making that effort, and the best reward is that provided by the reading material itself, by books which are at least meaningful, and at best funny or exciting. It is at this stage of beginning reading that attitudes towards reading and books are formed, attitudes which may shape future reading habits – or nonreading habits.

Criteria for selecting reading schemes and other books: the case for reappraisal

The task of appraising all the reading materials in the school in the light of a coherent set of criteria is central to the development of a language and reading policy. Such criteria should be discussed and agreed by the head and staff of each individual school. The following list constitutes, in my opinion, a minimum of what is needed to guide the selection of appropriate reading materials.

a)   The text must have meaning *for the child*

b)   The language should sound like the spoken language familiar to the child

c)   The interest level, *for the child*, should be high

d)   Illustrations should relate closely to the text and provide cues to its meaning

e)   There should be variety of stories of the kind children enjoy (funny, exciting, etc.)

Because most reading schemes lack any real interest for the children and provide a poor reading 'diet', some reading specialists wish to banish all basic reading schemes from the classroom, and use in their place story books: children's literature of as high quality and motivational value as possible. There is something to be said for this point of view, but to teach reading without the support of a structured scheme demands a great deal of the teacher's knowledge of children's literature, organizational ability, and not least, of willingness to spend a lot of time classifying and organizing reading materials.

Certainly, pupils should not be constrained or confined within too narrow boundaries by the reading scheme. They should not be forced to crawl on all fours through a reading scheme if they are capable of running through the fields of children's literature. Each individual child must be catered for and given scope for accelerated progress whenever that is possible.

For most teachers, reading schemes provide, however, a necessary framework within which they can plan a structured approach to reading with a reasonable expenditure of time and effort. Assuming that sufficient structure exists within the individual scheme, books and supplementary materials will fall naturally into a skills ladder system with its allied record-keeping approach.

Whatever kinds of materials are used, reading schemes, story books, teacher-made materials, etc., all materials must be carefully appraised in light of the criteria agreed by the head and staff of the school. And teachers must be prepared to act in accordance with the outcome of the appraisal. There is, for example, little point in concluding that a particular set of materials is unsuitable for beginning readers if one then goes on using them. Materials that do not come anywhere near meeting the agreed criteria for good reading materials *must be rejected*. Or, to put this in more positive terms, only materials that meet certain minimum demands should be used at all in the teaching of reading.

In addition to a set of criteria that makes it possible to specify 'minimal educational standards' for reading materials, each school will need a stategy for action vis-à-vis these materials. Such a strategy should include the following major steps:

a) the firm decision to stop using all materials that do not meet what the head and staff have agreed upon as 'minimum educational standards'

b) careful assessment of what is available in the market before any decisions are made about major purchases

c) a coordinated, rather than piecemeal, approach to the buying of materials, so that resources are not spent on a number of small purchases on 'impulse', leaving little or nothing for carefully planned purchases of larger sets of materials

d) the committment to choose, whenever there is a choice, the materials which *on balance* come closest to meeting all the criteria for selection

e) the utilizing of every opportunity to convey to publishers and publishers' representatives information about what kinds of materials are needed – and what kinds are not acceptable.

There exists no 'perfect' reading scheme or other set of reading materials that would suit all groups of children all the time. But some schemes are much better than other schemes, judged by the kind of criteria presented earlier, and there are schemes on the market which use a minimum of 'primerese' and which offer meaningful and potentially stimulating content. By consistently using schemes of this kind and refusing to put up with the 'primerese', heads and teachers will create an increasing demand for better reading materials. And this demand will stimulate authors and publishers to produce more meaningful and exciting reading books and fewer books that are 'not about anything'.

CHAPTER 7

ASSESSING AND MONITORING PUPIL PROGRESS

Informal and formal assessment of reading ability

A systematic approach to instruction always implies that there are well-defined objectives which govern the process of instruction and that there are means of assessing whether, or to what extent, the different objectives have been achieved. The language and reading curriculum described earlier (Chapter 6) involves the teacher in a continuous monitoring of each individual child in his progress through graded levels of the curriculum organized in ladders. This monitoring presupposes a large number of informal assessments, where the teacher judges, on the basis of her experience, whether the child has mastered a particular skill or whether further learning or practice is needed.

Informal assessment, based on the teacher's professional judgement, will always remain one of the most important forms of assessment in the field of beginning reading. Through listening to children reading, and through talking to them about what they have read, the teacher can identify strengths and weaknesses in each child's reading skills. This approach to assessment can be somewhat more structured and formalized by means of an Informal Reading Inventory (see e.g., Pumfrey 1976). This is based on a series of graded passages with questions aimed at establishing how much a child has understood of each passage. An Informal Reading Inventory usually also takes into account the number and nature of the child's oral reading errors.

Another structured approach to the teacher's own assessment is Miscue Analysis (Goodman 1973), which leads to a diagnosis of the reader's strengths and weaknesses through an analysis of the nature rather than the frequency of his misreadings or 'miscues', as the Goodmans call them.

The strength of the Informal Reading Inventory, Miscue Analysis, and similar approaches to assessment is that they allow the teacher to select the reading material used for the purpose of assessment, so that she can be sure to use only texts which are suitable for *her* pupils. Children's reading skills can thus be assessed on the same kind of material as they have been using in developing and training these skills. And it can be ensured that the texts used for assessment purposes are sufficiently motivating.

Standardized tests of reading skills do not have these advantages. A standardized test consists of a given text which is the same for all children. This text may not be equally suitable for all classes, even if test authors make great efforts to select texts with very wide appeal. But standardized tests have another extremely important advantage which informal methods do not have. They provide the teacher with a frame of reference for the assessment of individual children, so that the ability of each child can be evaluated against a national norm or standard.

The teacher can monitor the progress of each child by means of informal assessment, but only a standardized test can tell her how well her children are doing compared to the average for large representative groups of children from all over the country. Standardized tests are therefore essential as a complement to the teacher's own informal assessment.

What aspects of reading should we assess?

It has already been pointed out that instruction in the field of language and reading, as well as in any other field, must be governed by well-defined objectives. The question of what aspects to assess should then depend upon the nature of the objectives, since the main purpose of assessment is to find out to what extent the objectives have been achieved.

When reading is seen as a language and communication process, it becomes natural to focus the assessment on the factor which primarily determines whether or not communication has occurred as the results of reading, that is on *comprehension*. This may seem obvious, since everybody would agree that successful reading of a text presupposes that the 'message' of the text has been understood. It is surprising, however, how often reading ability is tested in a way which does not ensure that the reader has understood what he has read. For example, a test battery published in Britain in 1972, Assessment of Reading Ability, tests seven different reading skills, but none of these seven skills is directly concerned with comprehension (Pumfrey 1976). And widely used reading tests for the infant stage, e.g., Schonell Graded Word Reading and Burt Graded Vocabulary Test, only measure the ability to recognize and pronounce isolated words.

Even when it has been agreed that assessment of reading ability should focus on comprehension, it still remains to be determined exactly how comprehension can best be assessed. A commonly used method of assessing comprehension is to let the pupils read a text and then give them – orally or in writing – a series of 'comprehension questions'. Sometimes ten questions are given after a test and comprehension is expressed as a percentage: seven questions answered correctly out of ten gives '70 percent comprehension' and so on. One obvious problem with this approach is that the difficulty of the task depends as much on the questions as on the difficulty of the passage read. One can ask easy questions about a relatively difficult text, and difficult questions about an easy text. To answer ten out of ten easy questions does in no way guarantee '100 percent comprehension'.

Another weakness in the 'comprehension question' approach is that it is often possible to answer the questions without having read the text, particularly if they are mutliple-choice questions, where the pupil has to choose one of four or five alternative answers. Comprehension questions can easily become questions about general knowledge or general verbal intelligence, testing not how much the reader has understood of the text, but how much he knew or understood beforehand.

The most important alternative to comprehension questions is the so-called 'cloze procedure'. Since this approach is not as widely used, a more detailed discussion of its nature and merits follows.

Cloze procedure and comprehension

Cloze procedure involves the regular deletion of single words in a passage of meaningful flowing prose in order that an attempt can be made by the reader to replace the missing words, either exactly or by synonyms.

Cloze procedure may be used to evaluate the difficulty level of the reading material or to evaluate the reader's degree of understanding of the material, that is, the reader's comprehension of it. It is with the latter use of cloze procedure that we are concerned here. The main issue is whether cloze procedure provides a valid measure of comprehension in reading, and hence a valid measure of reading ability or attainment.

Rankin (1962) and Jenkinson (1957) investigated cloze procedure in relation to reading comprehension. Rankin concluded that cloze is a valid measure of general reading comprehension, and Jenkinson, working with American high school pupils, reported high correlations between cloze test scores and 'vocabulary' and 'level of comprehension' subtests.

Bormuth (1967) constructed tests to measure the comprehension of vocabulary, explicitly stated facts, sequences of events, inferences, casual relationships, main idea, and author's motive, in each of nine passages. He gave these and the cloze readability tests to American children of junior school age, and the correlations between the cloze and conventional tests over each passage ranged from .73 to .84. When the correlations of the tests were corrected for unreliabilities of the tests, the correlations approached 1.00, i.e., perfect correlation, meaning that the tests compared measure virtually the same thing.

In summary, Bormuth found that cloze tests are good predictors of ability to score on comprehension skills like vocabulary meaning, understanding facts, seeing relationships, and drawing inferences. However, there is little evidence to suggest that a teacher could put much reliance on cloze test results to predict the ability to get the *main idea* in the content materials used. (This finding is confirmed by an international study by Grundin *et al.*, 1978). Of particular interest to this study is Bormuth's finding that cloze tests are: 'appropriate for use with individuals and groups which vary very widely in comprehension ability'.

Ransom (1968) has conducted several studies from which she concludes that standardized reading tests overestimate children's instructional levels. She began to use the Informal Reading Inventory technique, with questions directed to test some of the recognized comprehension skills, e.g., main ideas, inference, sequence of events, etc. She compared this approach with the results of cloze tests in the same passages, and correlations were high.

The Informal Reading Inventory depends for its usefulness on the content and meaningfulness of the text being tested. The early books of most reading schemes do not support this approach, because of the severely restricted vocabulary and high degree of repetition encountered in the early readers. The nature of the language involved is often so unlike any form of spoken language that the construction of a cloze test would be quite impossible. I am referring to passages such as:

Come, Peter, come,

See, Peter, see,

Come, play ball

Come play Peter

Come, come, come,

Peter and Pat play ball.

Any attempt to derive meaningful results from either cloze or Informal Reading Inventory testings based on the very great majority of first- or second-level readers is doomed to failure.

Simons (1971) criticizes seven major approaches to reading comprehension – the skills approach, readability approach, factor analytical approach, introspective approach, measurement approach, correlational approach, and models approach. He claims that the common weakness is the lack of theoretical knowledge of the process of reading and of reading comprehension – thereby separating the two concepts into decoding and comprehension. Simons suggests a new direction based on linguistic theory and psycholinguistic research. His discussion of traditional reading comprehension tests and cloze tests concludes that

> The cloze test may be a better measure of comprehension because it is measuring fewer extraneous aspects of cognitive functioning than traditional tests do. Quite obviously traditional and cloze comprehension have face validity and are measuring indirectly the reading comprehension process. (p.348)

To be useful in educational practice, a diagnostic teaching or testing device must not only be theoretically well founded, but also a practical proposition in terms of teacher involvement and time consumption. Cloze procedure has shown itself to be manifestly advantageous with regard to both these criteria.

My review of the literature on comprehension and cloze procedure gave ample evidence for the superiority of cloze procedure as a means of measuring the ability to read for meaning. I therefore decided to construct for the purpose of evaluating the language and reading curriculum described in this book a cloze test for children reaching the end of their infant schooling (normally children approaching seven years of age).

Cloze procedure provides a measure of reading ability which is highly consistent with the psycholinguistic view of reading. It also provides a practical and economical means of measuring reading attainment. Furthermore, a standardized cloze test of reading ability should, indirectly, constitute a valuable inservice teacher training tool. Using such a test, teachers may more easily recognize the importance of confronting their young pupils with motivating, meaningful reading materials, and of encouraging them to use psycholinguistic guessing-game techniques as a means of deriving meaning from a text.

The implications of cloze procedure concerning changes in teacher's attitudes, and hence practices, vis-à-vis the teaching of reading are important. If the pupils require 'guessing-game' skills in order to perform well on a prescribed test, teachers are more likely to help their pupils to become efficient in using the necessary techniques. This can be regarded as 'teaching to the test', something which is often regarded as poor teaching.

There is, however, nothing wrong *per se* in 'teaching to the test'. If, as in this case, it leads to the development in the pupils of sound reading strategies, it must be regarded as a desirable outcome.

The Hunter Cloze Test

The most important – and also the most difficult – task in the construction of a cloze test is that of writing the text on which to base the test. The text must be suitable in terms of language difficulty, interest level, and length. With these criteria in mind, I wrote three simple stories: one about a dragon called Grump, one about a small boy who lost his bike, and one about a girl in a supermarket buying food for her birthday party. I read these stories to several classes. Some of my student teachers helped me at this stage by reading the stories to their classes and noting pupil reactions.

'Grump', the story about the dragon, proved to be the unanimous favourite. This story was then rewritten in order to make the language as simple as possible and revised after more field testing. The final version of the story consists of 12 sentences with a total of 144 words. In the cloze test based on this text the first sentence is left intact, in order to help the pupils to understand quickly what the story is about. Starting from the beginning of the second sentence there is a total of 32 deletions.

Preliminary administrations of the test had indicated that the length of the test was appropriate for seven-year-olds, and that the test was sufficiently taxing for the brighter children to obviate any 'ceiling' effect.

In the printed version of the Hunter Cloze Test every deleted word is replaced by a line of uniform length, on which the child writes down his response. The maximum time allowed for any child to complete the test was ten minutes. The children were given the following instructions orally:

> This is a story about a dragon called Grump.
>
> The story has lots of words missing. Where a word has been missed out, a line has been put in its place.
>
> To play the game *you* have to put *one* word on *each* line so that the story makes sense. You must only write one word on each line.
>
> If you can't think of a word, read the rest of the sentence, and that will help you to guess what the missing word is. If you still can't think of the word, leave it out and go on to the next missing word.
>
> If you want to change one of your answers, cross out the word you've written, and write the new word neatly up above the line.
>
> When you've written all the missing words you can finish the story on the back of the paper.
>
> Don't look at anybody else's story because that spoils the game.
>
> Look at your story and listen, while I read the first sentence to you. Now read the first sentence *with* me – all together.
>
> Now, on you go, with your lips closed, and fill in as many of the missing words as you can.

Encouraging the children to 'finish the story' when they have completed the actual cloze test is partly a device to keep fast-working children occupied during the ten-minute period. But this additional task also makes it possible for the teacher to identify children with unusually high reading and writing ability, and helps to make her aware of the potential creative writing ability of those pupils who complete the test and reach that stage.

Cloze tests are often scored by giving one point for every correct word filled in, i.e., every word that agrees exactly with the original text. This makes the scoring quick and easy, and it seems to be an adequate method for scoring cloze tests for older children (see e.g., Bormuth 1969). With very young children I consider it to be important to give the child credit for every response that 'makes sense', even if it is not a factually correct response. The scoring of the Hunter Cloze Test is therefore achieved by giving one point for every word (filled in by the child) which 'makes sense' in the context of the passage. Obviously, there are some cases where judgements as to what 'makes sense' become somewhat subjective.

The reliability of the Hunter Cloze Test has been estimated to be 0.93, which indicates that the test has a very high reliability.

Assessing children's attitude to reading

When reading is regarded as a meaningful, purpose-oriented activity, and part of a communication process, children's motivation becomes an important aspect in the teaching of reading. To be a reader means not only to be able to read, but also to want to read. Well-developed reading skills are of little value if the child's attitude to books and reading is such that he will read only when he feels that he *has* to, but never of his own free will.

Some means of assessing children's attitude to reading is an important complement to the methods of assessing ability which have already been discussed. As part of my attempt to evaluate an experimental language and reading curriculum empirically, I therefore decided to develop a simple attitude test which could be administered to infant school children and reveal something about their attitudes to reading.

The whole attitude test incorporated questions about various school and out-of-school activities including reading. The purpose of this was to try to make the test seem like a game, where the children replied spontaneously to a number of questions and thus revealed their 'true' likings. If the children had simply been asked whether they liked reading, some of them may have made positive responses because they felt that they were expected to like it. The inclusion of a variety of attitude questions – some concerning things most children are known to like, and some concerning things they tend to dislike – also made it possible to check that the children revealed their attitude by indicating great liking for some things and less liking for others.

One of the most difficult problems in developing this attitude test for infant school children was to find a suitable way of illustrating different degrees of liking. Attitudes tests for adults or older children usually contain questions like 'Do you enjoy doing such and such thing . . .

Very much,

A great deal,

Not very much, or

Not at all?'

In a group test for young children, response alternatives of this kind could easily be confusing, and with children who have just begun to learn to read they would be impossible to use.

After trying various alternative ways of illustrating degrees of liking, I preferred a simple and effective way, which I believe is an innovation in this area – the 'funny faces'. Three degrees of liking, positive, neutral/indifferent, and negative are illustrated by the shape of the mouth in the drawing of a 'funny face' as shown below.

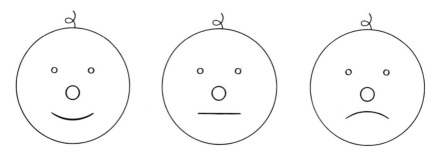

For each item in the attitude test, a row of three 'funny faces' was printed, and the children were asked to indicate their degree of liking by marking a line under the appropriate face. Before the test, it had been explained to them that one face meant '*like*', one meant '*does not like*', and the one in the middle meant '*no* feelings of like or dislike' – 'don't really care one way or the other'. The children enjoyed these faces very much, and they quickly grasped the principle of how to express liking or disliking by marking a 'funny face'. Because this attitude test uses oral instructions in combination with drawings on a test sheet given to each individual child, it can be used with infant school pupils of all ability levels, including the nonreaders. The fact that it is a group test makes it attractive from the point of view of testing time. A whole class can be assessed in a fraction of the time it would take to assess each pupil's attitudes individually. The group testing can have one further advantage, compared with individual assessment, in that it gives the child a certain degree of anonymity. Not that the teacher does not know how each child replies, but so that the child does not have to express his attitude 'face-to-face' with the teacher. Some children, who have a negative attitude to certain school activities, may, even at the infant stage, be sufficiently sophisticated to realize that their attitude is not what the teacher would like it to be. These children may feel more free to express their attitudes in a group test game situation. Observations made by myself and by class teachers during a number of testing sessions satisfied us that children understand the task involved in the Attitude Test, and that practically all children complete it accurately in a way which reflects their real feelings.

Assessment of spoken language and writing

The approach to language and literacy development proposed in this book is one which emphasizes the intimate relation between language, on the one hand, and literacy, on the other. It is consequently important to try to assess all the major aspects of language and literacy development. So far this chapter on assessment has mainly dealt with reading, and with comprehension – the most important outcome of the reading process. That is, it has dealt mainly with the *receptive* side of language and literacy, with children's ability to receive and understand language produced by others.

It is natural that the assessment of reading is very much in the focus of attention during the period of beginning reading, when children acquire – or, in some cases, fail to acquire – the fundamental receptive communication skill of reading for meaning. This must, however, not lead to the neglecting of the *productive* side of language and literacy, that is of *speaking* and *writing*. If the receptive and productive aspects of language communication are to develop jointly, there is surely a need for assessment of both aspects.

Unfortunately, the assessment of the productive aspects of language communication poses even greater problems than the assessment of the receptive aspect. We have well-developed and tested methods for measuring children's ability to comprehend (some of these have been discussed earlier in this chapter), but there are no equivalent methods for measuring the ability to produce language through speaking or writing. We can easily measure the *quantity* of language produced in a given situation, e.g., the number of words in an written essay or in an oral description of a picture. But a child's level of language development is usually not directly reflected in the quantity of his spoken or written language, although quantity of written language within a time limit can say a great deal about the ease or fluency with which a child writes.

The most important aspects of children's 'language production' are to be found in various *qualitative* features. To what extent does the child convey his ideas so that others can understand them? To what extent can he use language imaginatively and creatively? These are the kinds of questions that any attempt to assess children's speaking and writing must address.

As long as we do not have access to any objective measures of quality in spoken or written language, assessment in these areas will have to rely on the best available expert judgement, i.e., the judgement of the teacher. It has been established, however, that even experienced teachers show considerable disagreement when they are asked to judge the overall or 'global' quality of a piece of language production (see e.g., Rowntree 1977, Chapter 6, where unreliability in essay grading is discussed). Teacher ratings can be much improved if they are focused on a number of aspects or dimensions of quality, rather than on just the one aspect of 'global quality'. Examples of such dimensions of quality in young children's productive language skills are:

intelligibility (i.e., clarity of enunciation in the case of spoken language and legibility in the case of written language)

fluency (i.e., the ease with which the child 'produces' language)

confidence (in expressing himself orally, something which is closely related to 'fluency')

imagination and *originality* (i.e., aspects of the ability to go 'beyond what is given' in describing events)

accuracy (i.e., the degree to which the language used describes situations and events, interprets relationships, etc. precisely and accurately)

All of these aspects of language skills can – and should – be assessed informally by the teacher on the basis of the children's spoken and written language as part of a regular diagnostic teaching approach. As a complement to the continuous informal assessment, there is, however, also a need for more formal procedures where children are assessed in relatively uniform or 'standarized' situations. For example, spoken language can be assessed by means of showing the child a picture which is quite rich in detail and which is likely to be appealing to the child. The child is asked to tell what is happening in the picture, and the teacher then rates his spoken language performance in a specified set of aspects like the ones listed earlier. If a fairly large number of children are given exactly the same task, the spoken language performance of each child can be rated in relation to what is normal for children of his age group.

Another type of 'language production task' that can be given to all children is one which entails asking the child to describe or relate something of which all children have a great deal of experience, e.g., 'what is happening on the way to school?' or 'what do you see on the way to school?' Such a task can be used either for the assessment of spoken language or for the assessment of written language.

It can be argued that tasks of the kind described here assess not only the child's language skills, but also his degree of knowledge and experience in different areas. This is undoubtedly true, but I would argue that it is equally true about any test of productive language skills. A child's ability to use language is to a large extent a function of his experience and 'understanding' of the world around him. To assess the ability to communicate through language must therefore always build on the assumption that there is something which can be communicated, that the child has at least some knowledge and experience which he can try to express verbally. We can try to ensure, through the careful choice of suitable 'assessment situations', that all children are given a fair chance to demonstrate their skills. But if a child has nothing – or very, very little – to express, there is no way in which we can assess his ability to express himself. My experience with language games at the nursery and infant levels has shown, however, that it is extremely rare that young children have nothing to express verbally if proper stimulation has been given. Their knowledge and experience of their immediate environment is practically always such that they 'have something to say', although the ability to express it verbally varies enormously from child to child.

The assessment of spoken language using 'standardized assessment situations' is time-consuming, since it has to be done individually, listening to one child at the time. To assess written language is by comparison very much easier, since it can be organized as a 'group assessment'. It would, however, be very unfortunate if teachers were to neglect the regular assessment of spoken language simply because it is felt to be too time-consuming. Many children are slow in developing the level of literacy which permits them to express themselves relatively freely in writing. Other children are inhibited by their uncertainty about the correct spelling of many of the words they would like to use in their writing. And, of course, the task of actually putting the words on paper in a legible hand can be an inhibiting factor for those children who do not have highly developed motor skills of the kind needed for handwriting.

It is, then, particularly important that the development of spoken language is assessed for all those children who for various reasons are handicapped or inhibited in the writing task. Only when both spoken and written language skills have been assessed is it possible to determine if lack of progress in written language is due mainly to poor *language skills generally* or if it is due to poor *writing ability*.

During the period 1973-1975 I carried out an empirical evaluation of the language and reading curriculum presented and discussed in this book. A detailed description of this evaluative study is given in the following chapter. There was no funding or working-time allocation for the study, and these constraints necessitated a concentration of the assessments that could be undertaken to only a small number of variables.

The assessment focused on the educational outcomes of the experimental curriculum as they were reflected in reading progress and in attitudes to reading. The most serious limitation of my evaluative study was undoubtedly the absence of evaluation of the closely related and equally important skills of spoken language and writing. (The problems involved in assessing spoken language development have been discussed in Chapter 3, and also earlier in this chapter.)

Clearly, spoken language, being the principal mode of communication throughout adult life, needs to be continuously monitored, and its development needs to be systematically promoted in a diagnostic teaching programme for all children.

In response to this need for assessment of a whole range of aspects of language and literacy development, I decided to utilize the experiences from my evaluation study and from my classroom work in a large number of schools for the purpose of developing a more comprehensive series of assessment instruments. The two tests described earlier in this chapter, the Hunter Cloze Test and the Hunter Attitude Test, have been further revised and supplemented by instruments for the assessment of spoken language, free writing, and spelling. The resulting test battery, Level One of the *Hunter-Grundin Literacy Profiles*, is one of the most important outcomes of my experimental work. The instruments have been extensively field-tested and standardized for use in the infant school and with first-year pupils in the junior school. They are available from The Test Agency, Cournswood House, North Dean, High Wycombe, Buckinghamshire.

Continuous assessment, recordkeeping, and diagnostic teaching

Assessment in the classroom, whether informal or formal, is never an end in itself; it is always a means for the furthering of educational aims and objectives. Assessment must therefore be carefully planned as part of the comprehensive, systematic approach to language and literacy advocated in this book. The planning of assessment should involve not only decisions about what kind of assessment should be undertaken and when it should be done, but also decisions about how the outcome of assessments should be utilized in teaching.

It has been emphasized earlier in this chapter that there is a need for both informal and formal methods of assessment in the infant school classroom. All methods of assessment have at least one thing in common: they result in educationally relevant *information about individual pupils*, which is *recorded* for future reference. The design of a recordkeeping system which is easy to operate and which can become an effective instrument in the organization of classroom work is, therefore, a vital part of the assessment process.

A 'policy' for language and literacy of the kind highly recommended by the Bullock Report (DES 1975) must, then, contain not only a comprehensive, systematic curriculum, but also assessment procedures with accompanying procedures for recordkeeping and for the utilization of recorded assessment results in a process of *diagnostic teaching*. The concept of diagnostic teaching is neither new nor revolutionary. It implies simply that teaching is always aimed at starting *'where the child is'* and that there is a commitment to incorporate in the teaching process an organized, continuous effort to find out 'where the child is' before any new phase of teaching/learning is started.

If each teacher has a very small number of pupils and if she can remain their teacher for quite a long period of time, diagnostic teaching can probably be organized in an informal way, on the basis of a stable personal relationship where the teacher is constantly aware of the 'learning status' of each child. In such a situation it is even likely that the teacher's memory will provide an adequate 'recordkeeping system'.

We all know, however, that the reality of the infant school is different: each teacher is responsible for a large group of children and 'turnover' of staff is high in many schools. A continuous process of diagnostic teaching is therefore impossible without assessment which results in information that can be – and *is* – recorded.

The recordkeeping system for an individual school must be determined by the head and staff of that school, in the light of their knowledge of the pupil population of the school and the particular needs within that population. With the possible exception of very small schools with low turnover of staff, each school will need records at two different levels:

a)   records at *classroom level*, kept by the class teacher according to principles agreed for the whole school

b)   records at *school or 'interschool' level*, which may be kept by class teachers, but which are under the direct supervision of the head of the school

Records at *classroom level* guide the diagnostic teaching on a week-by-week, or even day-by-day, basis. It may not be possible to make these records uniform for all teachers and all classes, since they will reflect the teaching 'style' and classroom organization of the individual teacher. It should, however, be possible for each school to agree on the basic principles for recordkeeping at classroom level, and to develop record sheets that can be used throughout the school. In determining principles for recordkeeping and designing record sheets, the following points should be borne in mind:

1   Recorded information should provide a basis for the next stage of the teaching/learning process; the diagnostic teaching principle

2   The pattern of recording should reflect the systematic nature of the teacher's approach to the structuring and organizing of each child's learning experiences

3   The system should lend itself to 'on-the-spot' recording of all relevant 'events', e.g., individual or group reading experiences or language game experiences

4   Record sheets should be designed in a way which facilitates their use

5   Although designed for the use of one teacher, records should be sufficiently explicit to be of use to another teacher who is taking over the class
temporarily or permanently

The records at classroom level may prove too detailed for the purpose of
providing an overview of the progress made by the school's pupil population as a whole, or by all pupils in a particular age group. Such records may
also be too detailed for the purpose of 'briefing' another school to which a
pupil is being transferred. The head of a school will therefore need to have
access to this second kind of record at 'school' or 'interschool' level. These
should contain information derived mainly from formal assessment at
regular intervals – not less than once a year. If the records kept by the
individual teacher serve the needs of diagnostic teaching, the 'school
records' should serve the needs of *diagnostic management*, i.e., of management of all the resources in terms of money, materials, staff, etc. available to
the individual school with a view to ensuring the best possible progress for
all the children.

Since the school records of pupil progress are to serve the purpose of
providing information about pupils when they are transferred from one
school to another, it is desirable that there is a certain degree of uniformity
from school to school in the recordkeeping system. It seems particularly
important that there should be uniformity within each LEA. This would
not only facilitate transfers from school to school, it would also make the
records very useful to the LEA in its planning, allocation of resources to
schools, and so on.

The Hunter-Grundin Literacy Profiles, which where briefly mentioned in
the previous section, provide an example of how a system for continuous
assessment and recordkeeping at what is here called 'school level' can be
organized. The profiles contain instruments for annual assessment of pupil
progress in the most important aspects of language and literacy, and a folder
in which to keep all the test papers is provided. The folder also serves as a
cumulative record where information about the individual pupil's progress
over several years can be registered. The kind of information summarized in
this cumulative record can be seen in the facsimile of the front of the folders
in Figure 3.

Figure 3

School	Hunter–Grundin Literacy Profiles Cumulative Record

Time of assessment: Year
Month

☐ ☐ ☐ ☐ ☐

Pupil's age ....

☐ ☐ ☐ ☐ ☐

SPOKEN LANGUAGE
(teacher ratings)

Confidence .... ☐ ☐ ☐ ☐ ☐

Enunciation .... ☐ ☐ ☐ ☐ ☐

Vocabulary .... ☐ ☐ ☐ ☐ ☐

Accuracy .... ☐ ☐ ☐ ☐ ☐

Imagination .... ☐ ☐ ☐ ☐ ☐

READING
Reading for meaning:

Reading age .... ☐ ☐ ☐ ☐ ☐

Standard score .... ☐ ☐ ☐ ☐ ☐

Enjoyment of reading:

Pupil's rating .... ☐ ☐ ☐ ☐ ☐

Teacher's rating .... ☐ ☐ ☐ ☐ ☐

WRITTEN LANGUAGE
  Spelling

Standard score .... ☐ ☐ ☐ ☐ ☐

Free writing (teacher ratings)

Legibility .... ☐ ☐ ☐ ☐ ☐

Fluency .... ☐ ☐ ☐ ☐ ☐

Accuracy .... ☐ ☐ ☐ ☐ ☐

Originality .... ☐ ☐ ☐ ☐ ☐

Name:

Sex:

Date of Birth:

CHAPTER 8

EVALUATING THE CURRICULUM THROUGH ACTION RESEARCH

The importance of action research

To mark the closing of the tenth year of the *Reading Research Quarterly*, an editorial was published reflecting on the state of the art of reading research (*Reading Research Quarterly* 1974-1975, No. 4). The editors pointed out that each year the journal reviews a number of well-designed, carefully implemented and precisely documented studies related to reading, but that regrettably few of these studies make a contribution towards our understanding of the ways in which children learn to read. It follows that few of them help us to do a better job of teaching reading in the classroom. It is described as 'disconcerting' that so many of these studies are both 'myopic' and narrow in scope and that they frequently fail to address themselves to the most important issues and concerns related to the teaching and learning situations. It would appear that researchers, although they know the issues and problems in the field, respond by developing ever more elaborate research designs and methods for statistical analysis of their data. But contacts with researchers have revealed that they themselves lament the fact that their sophisticated designs have failed to enable them to make more important contributions to the field of reading.

The editors of the *Reading Research Quarterly* ask why this is so. They ask what has brought about a situation in which researchers do not appear to have the tools, techniques, methodologies, and approaches to help them to study the important problems in the field of reading, and they suggest that the answer may lie in a phenomenon which they call 'methodological incarceration'. It is postulated that this state has been reached when research and investigation are restricted by traditional concepts which dictate what research is and how a research study should be designed, and when methodological considerations seem to dictate what questions are studied.

In addressing themselves to the question of why the field of reading research appears to have become so enmeshed, the editors suggest the possibility that educational researchers have themselves been educated within the confines of traditional psychological research methodologies. The point is made that the major research journals publish studies which employ 'sophisticated statistics and elaborate, elegant designs' which most researchers may long to emulate, and that there may be pressure on them, conscious or unconscious, to match the erudite respectability of the scientists and experimental psychologists. The *Reading Research Quarterly* publishes mainly American research, and against that background the editorial discussed here proceeds in an attack that is primarily 'home-based' in its implications:

> This attitude is certainly conveyed to doctoral students. In many reading departments students are even encouraged to avoid some types of research, such as methods studies, because the acceptable research designs are not usable. At the same time doctoral candidates are enrolled in courses that expose them only to current statistical techniques, and they are encouraged to do statistically neat and clean dissertation research. It is easy to see how these students can quickly fall into the trap of considering a research design and a statistical analysis before delineating the hypothesis to be studied or before grappling with the rationale for conducting the study. Design aspects of the study become the primary concern, and thus the tail wags the dog. Doctoral students become the victims of methodological incarceration, and they carry it on to the next generation of students. . . .

> We are sorely in need of research designs and new approaches that allow variables to emerge from the situation being studied, that admit to a lack of answers and even to a lack of questions, that allow for study in a natural setting, and that provide for the researcher's biases as well as alternative interpretations.

The writers of the *Reading Research Quarterly* editorial point out that other disciplines like anthropology, law, and journalism are fields which have freed themselves of methodological trammels in their search for truth. They insist that they, the editors, are not advocating methodological anarchy, but a 'willingness to dare' and an 'openness to new ideas and sources of ideas', and pledge themselves to the active encouragement of innovatory, classroom-based research in the field of reading.

My evaluative study satisfies the criteria for worthwhile research outlined by the editors of the *Reading Research Quarterly*. The empirical work is classroom-based and child-centred, and the language and reading curriculum developed within this study has grown out of the needs and responses of the teachers and young pupils involved. Sophisticated methods of statistical data analysis are not rejected, but have been used only where they can contribute significantly to our understanding of certain complex phenomena.

It is worth pointing out that my work encompasses both innovatory development and applied research in the field of the infant school language and reading curriculum. This research-cum-development work has been carried out in natural school settings, and in collaboration with teachers and heads of schools. That is, it is an example of what is sometimes called 'action research', where the researcher actively tries to promote certain educational changes and then attempts to assess the effects of these changes as objectively as possible. The ultimate objective of such research is the implementation of ideas and findings in educational practice. It is in the nature of action research that the researcher is not a neutral, disinterested observer, as he is assumed to be in the classical research paradigm of the natural sciences.

The 'action researcher' tends to study the effect of educational innovations in which he believes. He must therefore constantly be aware of the danger of subjectivity, of bias due to preconceived ideas in the interpretation of his empirical findings. If the outcome of action research is positive, i.e., if the innovation is seen to be valuable, it could be interpreted as simply proving what one 'knew all the time'. But this is far from invalidating the significance of the result. *One of the most important functions of empirical research is to attempt to verify, in a controlled and systematic way, what we think we 'know' intuitively.*

The description of my evaluative study and its results, which follows in this chapter, is relatively detailed. The main reason for this is that it has a dual function: it tries to put the case convincingly for a particular approach to language and reading in the infant school, and it shows how action research can be carried out with a minimum of special resources, thanks to the high level of professionalism and enthusiasm among the participating teachers.

The experimental and control schools

It was agreed that the September 1973 intake of pupils in the two schools where the experimental curriculum had been developed should constitute the experimental group, to be monitored and assessed during their two years in the infant school. These children would have their progress guided by means of the systematized schemes of work in language development, prereading and early reading – a curriculum organized and prepared in the way which has been described earlier in the book. Unfortunately, the head of one of the experimental schools had staffing problems soon after the start of the project, and was therefore unable to implement the experimental curriculum. Although the head of this school was most reluctant to give up the experiment, the school could not be included as an experimental school. Since I had background data for the children, I decided to include them in later testings as part of the control group.

To assess the progress of the experimental group, it was necessary to locate a number of schools using the same reading schemes as the experimental school, but not in the structured, systematic way that characterizes the experimental programme. The senior infant inspector of the Inner London Education Authority selected three schools where the headmistresses were experienced and enthusiastic teachers of reading. The heads of these three schools agreed to participate in the evaluative study, and their September 1973 intake, together with that of the 'drop-out' experimental school mentioned above, formed the control group. It must be noted that there was no attempt at any time to 'match' groups of pupils with each other, or to 'match' teachers. The aim of the selection procedure was simply to involve schools, none of which was *untypical* in its general aims and ethos, and all of which gave a relatively high priority to the teaching of reading.

Since groups of five-year-olds in these five schools had to be individually tested at the beginning of the study, teachers in all the schools became aware of the fact that their children were taking part in an experiment. Such an awareness might affect the teaching in control schools, e.g., by making teachers more 'competitive', more anxious to show good results in the area covered by the experiment – that is, in the field of reading. In order to establish whether such an 'experimental awareness' effect occurred, it was decided to include three additional control schools, where no testing was carried out until the children were ready to be transferred to the junior school, at the age of seven. These three schools were also known to put emphasis on their teaching of reading programme. They were selected, after consultation with the ILEA Research and Statistics Unit, so that the social backgrounds of the pupils in the eight schools covered a wide range from lower working class to middle class. The heads and teachers in these schools were not aware of their pupils being included in the comparative study until the final testings started at the end of the second year, when the aims of the study were discussed before they agreed to the testing. Pretesting was limited to one class per school, mainly because of the extremely time-consuming nature of the individual testing that was necessary at this early age (five years). The experimental school class which was pretested was of about the same size as the pretested control classes, but a number of the children in the experimental class had nursery school experience. Since it was reasonable to assume that the nursery school experience had influenced these children's language development positively, and since no control class children had had such experience, it was decided to exclude the experimental class children with nursery school experience from the data analysis. The experimental group monitored by me personally consisted of 24 pupils, 15 of whom had no nursery school experience and were included in the pretested group. The total number of children pretested was 132.

The testing at age seven included not only pupils from three control schools not tested at the beginning of the study, but also groups of pupils in the experimental school and three of the original control schools which had not been tested initially. This means that the final testings included two categories of experimental school pupils and three categories of control school pupils, namely:

experimental school pupils initially tested and monitored throughout the infant school years

experimental school pupils taught according to the same experimental syllabus but *not* initially tested

control school pupils initially tested and monitored throughout the infant school years

control school pupils who were in the same schools as those pretested and monitored, but who were not pretested and monitored

control pupils from schools where *no* pupils were pretested or monitored.

Details about the number of children in the various groups involved are given in Appendix 3, Table 1.

Monitoring of classwork in comparative studies

The form this study has taken is far from uncommon. When the results of an educational innovation are to be evaluated, it is customary to administer some kind of pretest to both experimental and control groups, to introduce the new plan or programme in the experimental but not in the control group, and after a period of time, to retest both groups in order to assess the effect of the innovation. It is often found in such studies that there is little or no difference between the groups. This phenomenon occurred so frequently in American projects that it was made the subject of a study by Cross, Giaquinta, and Bernstein (1971). The school chosen for their study was in the process of introducing a new kind of teacher model – the teacher as the 'agent' or facilitator of learning. This was called the 'catalytic' teacher model. The staff of the school was briefed about the aims of the study and the pretesting was carried out. But in this case the researchers undertook a special study by observation, interview, and questionnaire, in order to find out to what extent the original plan – the adoption of the new 'catalytic' model of teaching – was being implemented. It was found that during the first few weeks of the experiment the new mode of teaching was gradually abandoned, and classroom practice reverted to the 'normality' of more formal teaching. The reasons suggested for this were the force of habit and tradition, the lack of new training of the teachers involved, the absence of appropriate new materials for the management of learning, traditional timetabling and examination procedures, and minimal support from the deputy headmaster, who suspected the new kind of teaching and was unsympathetic towards it.

The rather unfortunate tendency for researchers to stay away from the classroom may have several reasons. Many researchers lack relevant teaching experience, and they may therefore feel that they are not competent judges of what is going on in the classroom. Researchers can also feel that they would be accused of interfering in the 'interal affairs' of the schools participating in the research studies. Finally, and this is probably the most important reason, frequent observation of what is actually happening in the classes involved is very time-consuming, which in its turn usually makes it impossible to include a large number of classes in an experimental study.

If including a large number of classes in a research study means that these classes cannot be properly monitored throughout the study, the results may lack validity for the simple reason that although we eventually know what the results are, we do not know what kind of teaching/learning process produced these results. In other words, the *validity* of any experimental results must be ensured before it becomes meaningful to discuss to what extent the results can be generalized from the specific samples used to a larger population.

The best way of ensuring the validity of results is to monitor the participating groups regularly, so that any deviation from the initial experimental plan can be noted and taken into account in the later analysis of the data. This kind of monitoring through frequent observations is particularly important in a study of beginning reading instruction, where so much depends not only on what materials are used, but also on *how* they are used by the teachers in order to promote children's learning. In my study I therefore decided to put great emphasis on observations of the participating classes. Naturally, this decision put a severe limitation on the number of classes I could include in my study, but I was convinced that a carefully monitored small-scale study would lead to more valid results than a large-scale study with little or no monitoring of most of the participating classes.

My wide experience of infant school teaching made it easy for me to be accepted as a colleague by the heads and staff in the participating schools. I became a welcome, unannounced visitor in the experimental school as well as in the control schools. Since the very fact that a class is the object of observation by an 'outside' observer may affect both the teacher and the children – the so-called Hawthorne effect – I took great care to visit each of the four initial control schools as often as I visited the experimental school.

My observations in the experimental school primarily concerned the way in which the experimental language and reading syllabus was implemented throughout the two years covered by my study. In the control schools I was mainly interested in finding out what the approach was to the promotion of language development and to the teaching of beginning reading. My experiences from earlier observations of a very large number of infant schools had shown that a *systematic* and structured approach to language development was very rare indeed, and observations in the control schools confirmed this, although incidental opportunities for language development were used.

It is my conclusion that the general quality of education was of the same, high level in *all* the participating schools, and that the difference between the experimental school and the control schools was mainly one of different approaches to language and reading, that is, precisely the kind of difference I had set out to study.

Similarities and differences in the experimental and control schools

It is a feature of action research that the observations and judgements of participating teachers and researchers are given a high degree of importance. Discussion with all the headteachers and teachers involved in this study was, for me, the most valuable part of it, and it seems important to make clear in what ways the education of the pupils differed in the two categories involved (the experimental and the control schools). In fact, the difference was not great, and was not easily observable during visits. It was largely a difference in the underpinning *planning* and *organization* of the work in progress in the various schools.

In all cases the commonly accepted infant group activities prevailed, the kind which develop the various aspects of the education of young children. All classrooms contained a book corner, a 'shop', a Wendy house, and a variety of materials and equipment for painting, modelling, weighing, measuring, playing with sand and water, etc. In all cases there was at least one little animal, fish, or bird to be looked after, and growing flowers and plants were much in evidence. The children came together as a class for story time, singing, radio and television programmes, physical education, and religious assemblies (usually with the other classes in the school). At other times they were occupied in groups, with the activities of infant schooling.

All the teachers devoted a similar proportion of teaching time to reading (between 40 and 50 percent by the teachers' estimation), and individual pupils were *heard* reading from the appropriate book of their reading scheme as often as possible. In *all* schools opportunities for incidental language development were used in the normal context of the children's classroom activities.

The experimental school differed from the others in that there existed a planned, systematic curriculum for language and reading which had been worked out by the staff as a team, written down, graded, converted into schemes of work in 'ladder' sequences, and converted into individual pupil record sheets in this form (*see* Appendix 2).

The main observable difference was that the group activities in the experimental school regularly included groups, sitting around tables, playing language development games. These language games did not *replace* any of the usual games or activities, but merely *augmented* the provision to include games involving spoken language. Unquestionably, these language games, described in Chapter 6, were as appealing and enjoyable as any of the other activities.

The teachers using them were unanimous in their approval of them. It was generally agreed that the games provided very valuable additional opportunities for language development. Clearly, a teacher of some 25-30 small children cannot devote much time to the language development of individual pupils.

The teachers in the experimental school found that the individual pupil record sheets kept in ring binders made individualized instruction much more of a practical reality and facilitated diagnostic teaching. A glance at one pupil's record sheet for a given section of work gave a clear indication of how much he had and had not achieved, and it was much easier to ensure that no pupil was missing out or neglecting any part of the curriculum. All the teachers found that it was helpful to have a clear statement of a graded syllabus of activities through which pupils could be easily monitored. But it was observed by the more inexperienced teachers especially that this system provided welcome support.

Lastly, the experimental school teachers found that the agreed and planned statement of curriculum tended to necessitate the organization of some of the equipment, games, materials, and books into a *school resources bank*. This made *more* materials available to each class and hence individual pupil progress was never restricted or delayed.

Background data for the monitored classes

Background data collected and registered at the time when the children entered school include:

age of pupils at the time of testing

sex of pupils

social class status of pupils

Thackray Reading Readiness Score

General ability as measured by Thackray 'Draw-your-mummy' Test

The social class status of the pupils was determined on the basis of information about the occupation of each pupil's father or, in the case of most pupils from single parent families, his mother. The following social class categories were used:

lower working class (unskilled and semi-skilled)

upper working class (skilled)

middle class or 'non-working class' (professional, managerial, and highly skilled)

The Thackray Reading Readiness Profiles were used because they were the only tests for children of this age group which had been standardized for British children. They were not used for the purpose of predicting the pupils' stage of *readiness to read* (this topic has been critically discussed in Chapter 2), but only for the purpose of assessing their general development at the time of their entering school. The most useful part of the Thackray Profiles in this context is the fourth section, the 'Draw-your-mummy' Test. Research has shown that the degree of detail in children's drawings of human figures correlates with their general level of cognitive ability or maturity. The scoring involves a certain amount of subjective judgement, so in order to obtain reliable scores three colleagues helped by each scoring every drawing independently. Many infant school headteachers use this assessment task to obtain some indication of the capabilities with which new pupils arrive at school around their fifth birthday.

A summary of the background variables for the various groups is given in Appendix 3, Table 2.

Testing the 'top' infant classes (approximately seven-year-olds)

In July 1975, when the average age of the pupils was six years and eleven months, the final testings in the two-year study were carried out. As has been pointed out in the previous section, I considered it important to administer most tests individually on the previous test occasion because of the complexity of the tests and the age of the pupils. At this stage, however, it seemed much more appropriate to administer group tests. Both the experimental and the control group children were top infants, ready to transfer to junior school, and with two school years behind them.

In order to ensure uniformity of testing procedure, I decided to undertake all the testing in July 1975 myself. Although the children were old enough to be subjected to group tests of their reading ability, I regarded it as important to keep the group size fairly small. The exact number of children in each group which I tested depended upon the total number to be tested in the school, but the group size was never more than ten children.

A group of ten seven-year-olds is fairly easy to manage in a testing situation. The children can be brought close to the tester during the explanation of the nature of the 'games', as the tests were called when explained to the children. The proximity makes eye contact easier, and makes it relatively simple to observe each pupil's reaction to the instructions. It is also possible to observe, and hence to give additional explanation to, children who are slow to understand the nature of the task.

The same procedure of explaining the test task carefully, and checking that every child has understood, was followed in all the groups I tested. When I was satisfied that every child in the group was confident to cope with the test, the children were seated at desks from which they could not observe the work of any other pupil and were asked to complete the 'game'. If a pupil asked for some assistance during the test, I or the class teacher explained once more what was required of him, without giving the kind of specific help which would have invalidated the child's test result. The very great majority of the pupils coped privately and happily with the two tests administed at this stage. The tests administered at this final testing were The Hunter Cloze Test, and The Hunter Attitude Test.

The Hunter Cloze Test is described in detail in Chapter 7. This test was administered first to each of the groups, and the pupils were allowed a maximum time of ten minutes to complete it. The Hunter Attitude Test is also described in Chapter 7. This test was administered in each group, immediately after the cloze test, and included a question about the children's degree of liking of the cloze test.

The tests were presented to the children as games and were clearly acceptable and enjoyable. Very few children asked for individual help during the testing. The Hunter Attitude Test was particularly well received, appreciated, and executed, and the test item concerning their attitude to the Hunter Cloze Test demonstrated unanimous liking of the latter. Even those pupils who were clearly unsuccessful in their attempt to complete the Hunter Cloze Test claimed to have enjoyed attempting it.

The tests administered at the end of the second infant school year were, as has been pointed out earlier, administered to the entire group of top infants in the experimental school and the seven control schools. The total number of children tested at this stage was 526, including 132 children in classes which had been initially tested (two years earlier) and monitored throughout their infant school years, and 394 children in classes which had not been initially tested or monitored during those two years.

Background data for the total sample

'Reading readiness' scores were, as has been pointed out, not available for those classes which were not initially tested. I did, however, collect certain background data for these pupils, notably information about their sex and their social class background. All the classes included in the final testings can therefore be compared in terms of the percentage of boys and the percentage of 'working-class' children in each group. Of these two background variables, sex and social class, the latter is usually found to be more significant. Information about sex was included mainly to make it possible to check whether, as is often assumed, boys do less well on language and reading tasks than girls.

The background data for the groups included in the final testings are summarized in Appendix 3, Table 3.

It is worth pointing out that only two of the seven control schools have a higher proportion of 'working-class' children than the experimental school. And even these two schools have only slightly higher proportions of 'working-class' children: 79 and 78 percent as compared to 73 percent in the experimental school. In other words, none of the control schools had a markedly more 'working-class' population than had the experimental school.

This comparison of background data for the experimental group and for the entire control group shows that there is no reason to assume that the experimental group consisted of children who were more privileged in terms of social background than the control children. On the contrary, the proportion of 'non-working-class' children, who might be more experienced in terms of the kind of language used in schools than the working-class children, is somewhat higher in the control group than in the experimental group.

The effects of the monitored experimental curriculum

As has been explained earlier in this chapter, the design of the study was such that some comparisons could be attempted both between experimental and control groups, which had been tested prior to the study and carefully monitored for two years, and between larger experimental and control groups which had *not* been pretested or monitored. The results for the monitored and pretested groups are shown in Appendix 3, Table 3.

The overall effect of the experimental language and reading programme in the pretested and continuously monitored group was assessed by means of a highly complex method of statistical analysis, multifactorial analysis of covariance. This kind of analysis is particularly valuable when initial differences between groups, e.g., in 'reading readiness', may have influenced the final results. This analysis takes into account all the background variables (in this case age, sex, social class, Thackray Reading Readiness, and general ability), and provides the most accurate and 'fair' comparison between the different groups that can be made on the basis of the available data.

In this case, when we compare the reading test results in the experimental and the control groups, the adjustment means that we have ensured, as far as possible, that observed differences in achievement between experimental and control groups are due to the systematic language and reading syllabus used in the experimental group, and not to other factors.

The conclusion that can be drawn from these results concerning the effect of the experimental syllabus is very clear. The experimental class achieved much better results on the reading test used in the study.

The experimental group included in this first stage of the analysis was small, only fifteen children. It could be argued that the small number of children involved invalidates the result. That would be true if the result had shown *'no significant difference'* between the groups, something which is very common in educational research studies. If no difference is discovered, it may well be that there *is* a difference, but it is so small that it can be mistaken for so called 'error variation', i.e., a consequence of uncontrolled, random influences which have nothing to do with the experimental programme one wants to study. But when a comparison shows a statistically *significant difference* in spite of the fact that one of the groups compared was very small, this means that the difference must be *considerable, otherwise it would have not have been detected.*

The simple conclusion to be drawn is, then, that the systematic language and reading programme implemented and monitored in an infant school class for two years was highly successful.

It is difficult to judge how great the difference between two groups is, when it can only be expressed in a single test score and when we do not know what level of achievement a given test score represents. The mean scores for the experimental and control groups in this case should, however, give some indication of the magnitude of the difference. The control children scored on the average *4.1* on the Hunter Cloze Test, whereas the experimental group childred scored *14.2*. In other words, the difference in mean score is more than twice as big as the mean score for the control group. The control group mean is, in fact, so low that one may be justified in concluding that most of the control children were not adequately 'reading for *meaning*' when they left the infant school.

The effect of the experimental curriculum without monitoring

The previous section has shown very clearly that the systematic language and reading programme as implemented and continuously monitored in one experimental class was highly successful in developing the children's ability to read for meaning. Although careful monitoring of any experimental work is very important in this kind of research, it is also of great interest to see what results are achieved in groups that are not directly monitored. The results on the final reading tests for those groups which were not pretested and monitored permit such a comparison.

Table 4 in Appendix 3 summarizes the data for all those experimental and control group children who were not tested prior to the study and who were not monitored during the two-year experimental period. The most interesting data in this context are the Hunter Cloze Test mean scores for the different schools, and the mean for the group of six control schools. The experimental school children scored on the average 17.6 on this reading test, whereas the overall average for the control schools was only 8.5, i.e., less than half the score of the experimental group.

The scores for the groups discussed here, both experimental and control groups, are higher than the corresponding scores for the monitored experimental and control groups. It is difficult to know exactly what caused this difference, since we do not have any 'reading readiness' or general ability scores for these children. But it is worth noting that the difference between experimental and control group is approximately the same for these groups as for the monitored groups, namely 9.1 points on the Hunter Cloze Test for the nonmonitored groups and 10.1 points for the monitored groups. This suggests that the overall effect of the systematic language and reading curriculum was the same throughout the experimental school, regardless of whether the children had been directly monitored by me or not. The absence of the Hawthore effect in this case is less surprising when one takes into account the fact that the new curriculum was enthusiastically adopted by all members of staff in the experimental school. It was very much a *school policy*, and not restricted to the class under observation.

The comparison between the nonmonitored experimental and control groups discussed here leads, then, to the same general conclusion as the comparison between the monitored groups presented earlier. The systematic and structured language and reading programme implemented in the experimental school was highly successful in helping the children to learn to read for meaning.

The pupil's enjoyment of reading

The pupil's enjoyment of reading was measured by means of the Hunter Attitude Test, which has been described earlier. Over 75 percent of the experimental school children indicated in their answers to this attitude test that they liked reading. In the control schools the percentage of pupils who liked reading varied from school to school between 47 percent and 85 percent, with an average for all control schools of 60 percent. The proportion of children who liked reading was, then, higher in the experimental school than in the average control school.

The emphasis, in the experimental curriculum, on reading as a meaningful activity appears to have been successful, not only in terms of increased reading ability, but also in terms of increased enjoyment of reading.

The attitude to the cloze test was measured using the same scale as that used for attitude to reading. The proportion of children who like the cloze test was higher in the experimental school (74 percent) than in most control schools, and also higher than the average for the whole control group (68 percent). There is little relationship between the attitude to the cloze test and the attitude to reading in general. In the control school with the least positive attitude to reading, the attitude to the cloze test was considerably better than average. And in another control school, where attitude to reading was very positive, attitude to the cloze test was below average.

There is some indication of a relationship between the attitude to the cloze test, on the one hand, and the cloze test performance, on the other. The school with the least positive attitude to the test also had the lowest mean score and the school with the most positive attitude had the highest mean among the control schools. It is not possible to determine, though, whether children tend to have a more negative attitude to the test because they find it difficult, or whether they do less well because they like the test less. In any case the general reaction to the cloze test was very favourable.

The results of the attitude measurements indicate that attitude to reading varied greatly from school to school, but that the systematic programme of the experimental school resulted in an attitude which is better than the average for comparable schools. As regards the cloze test, the results indicate that, although attitudes to this test also varied from school to school, only 5 percent of the pupils registered any dislike for this test.

Reading ability and social background

The concept of social class is a highly complex one. Differences between 'working class' and 'middle class' are determined by life-style and economic situation as well as by historical factors. We must also remember that there are very great differences between people within the same social class. To label an individual family 'working class' or 'middle class' says very little about that particular family, since it may or may not be typical of its class. It becomes meaningful to talk about *class differences* only when we compare the *average* for one group with the *average* for another. Individual 'working-class' children may, for instance, do very well on reading tests, even better than the average 'middle-class' child. But it is nevertheless true that the average working-class child almost invariably scores lower on reading tests than the average middle-class child.

The children I studied were classified as belonging to the 'middle class', 'upper working class' or 'lower working class' on the basis of their fathers' occupation (or mother's occupation in cases of the few single-parent families). This is a 'crude' division, but it is sufficient for the purpose of establishing whether the experimental language and reading curriculum was beneficial for that category of children which is most likely to be at a disadvantage in terms of language development when they enter school, i.e., the 'working-class' children. This is not to say that all working-class children are disadvantaged with regard to language development. Many working-class homes provide a very good environment for early language development, but there are more 'working-class' homes than 'middle-class' homes which do not provide a great deal of stimulation *in the kind of language development which helps children to experience success in school*.

The division of pupils into 'working class' and 'middle class' is, then, useful for the purpose of *group comparisons*, in that it should make it possible to detect any tendency for the experimental curriculum to benefit – or not to benefit – these children who are most likely to experience problems in their language and reading development in school.

In the continuously monitored classes there was at the age of seven an interaction between the effect of the experimental programme and the children's social background. That is, the effect of the experimental programme seems to be different depending on the social class background of the children. In the control group the tendency is the familiar one with the 'middle-class' children doing better than the 'working-class' children, while there is little difference between 'lower working-class' and 'upper working-class' children. This tendency implies that those who are relatively privileged already in terms of their *kind* of language usage when they start school, i.e., most 'middle-class' children, also benefit most from the schooling they get. If such a trend prevails over a number of years, one would expect the gap between the more privileged and the less privileged to grow wider and wider as the children grow older. This in its turn could be interpreted to mean that differences between groups of children which are due to social class differences are perpetuated in the schools.

The most interesting, almost sensational, aspect of the results discussed here is the achievement of the 'working-class' children in the experimental group. Both upper and lower working-class children in this class performed, on the average, *better* than the middle-class children in the same class. That is, the traditional relation between working-class and middle-class achievement is reversed. This also means that although the experimental syllabus was successful for children of all social classes, it was *particularly successful for the 'working-class' children*. This finding relates to a small group of experimental school children only, but the fact that it is *statistically significant in spite of the small number* of subjects included in the analysis suggests that the magnitude of the effect is unusually great.

Another way of illustrating the good performance of the 'working-class' children in the experimental group is provided by the percentages of children in different subgroups who scored 0 on the Hunter Cloze Test. No child in the experimental group, whether working class or middle class, scored 0 on that test, while a substantial proportion of the control group children failed to score any points. A child who scores 0 on this reading-for-meaning test has clearly not yet grasped the basic function of reading (although he may *sound* as if he can read). Over 40 percent of the 'lower working-class' children in the control group were *in this sense* nonreaders (i.e., they were not reading with understanding) and even among the 'middle-class' control children we find 16 percent nonreaders in this sense. In the experimental group, however, there is not a single child who *by this definition* is a nonreader.

The effect of social class background in the nonmonitored sample

In view of the remarkable finding that the 'working-class' children in the continuously monitored experimental class did exceedingly well, it was, of course, interesting to see how the 'working-class' children succeeded in the larger nonmonitored experimental group.

As far as the control children are concerned there is little difference between the monitored and nonmonitored sample, i.e., there is a tendency for 'middle-class' children to do better than 'working-class' children. For the experimental group there is, however, a big difference between the two samples. The unmonitored experimental group shows a clear correlation between achievement in reading and social background. The 'middle-class' children did much better on the cloze test than the 'working-class' children, a finding in direct contrast to the result in the monitored experimental class, where the 'working-class' children succeeded better than the 'middle-class' children.

It may seem as if the finding for the larger unmonitored experimental group (that 'middle-class' children do better than 'working-class' children, as we have come to expect) totally contradicts, and therefore renders invalid, the earlier finding that the experimental programme was particularly beneficial for the working-class children. This is, however, not necessarily the case.

The following seems to me to be the best way of explaining these two somewhat confusing findings. The results of the smaller, continuously monitored experimental class show clearly that 'working-class' children *can*, under certain circumstances, make very good progress in their language and reading development. The results in this class also show that the usual trend of the 'middle-class' children 'streaking ahead' and widening the gap between the more privileged and the less privileged *can* be reversed, that this gap *can* be diminished, perhaps even closed, under certain circumstances. The systematic, structured language and reading syllabus implemented in the experimental school must have contributed greatly to the progress of the 'working-class' children. But this curriculum programme, however good it may be, is not enough to *guarantee* a narrowing of the gap between more privileged 'middle-class' children and less privileged 'working-class' children. Something more is needed.

Reading progress and 'restlessness'

In the experimental and control classes which I personally monitored, I was able to establish through my own observations that there were no remarkable differences between the groups with regard to the children's general classroom behaviour. In order to have access to some kind of information about the general classroom behaviour of the children in the unmonitored classes, I asked their teachers to rate each pupil's behaviour on a three-point 'restless' scale. The three alternatives on the scale were *'restless'*, *'average'*, and *'quiet'*.

The main reason for trying to establish how many children in each class could be described as 'restless' was that it could give an indication about the general 'climate' in which that class and its teacher worked. If a majority of the children in a class are restless, the working situation in that class must be very different from the situation in a class where children are described as 'quiet' or as 'average'. The proportion of restless children in the experimental group was *31 percent*, while the average for the whole control group was *23 percent* (see Appendix 3, Table 3.) The large majority of the children in both groups were, then, not described as restless, but as average or quiet. The experimental group had a somewhat higher proportion of restless children, but the difference was not large enough to be regarded as statistically significant.

Most teachers would probably expect a child's degree of restlessness to affect his learning, at least to some degree. The main reason for this expectation could in that case be that teachers generally find restless children more difficult to teach than quiet children. What is easily overlooked, though, is that the fact that a child is difficult to *teach* does not necessarily mean that the child *learns* less than the more 'easy-to-teach' children. The learning result will largely depend upon whether or not the teacher can overcome the difficulties, and provide learning experiences that suit the individual child.

In view of this discussion it is interesting to look at the correlation between restlessness and reading achievement in each type of school, experimental and control.

For the control group such an analysis shows the kind of correlation many teachers would expect: the restless children score lower than the 'average', and the 'average' score lower than the quiet children. That is, in the control classes there is a tendency for children to *learn more the easier they are to teach*. This suggests that teaching in those control classes was such that children were expected to be primarily *receptive* and *not* to any high degree *active*.

In the experimental group, on the other hand, there is the opposite trend. The children who were rated as 'restless' were the most successful readers, and the quiet children were, on the average, the least successful. This difference in trend between experimental and control group is *both statistically and practically significant*. It suggests that 'restlessness', which is normally regarded as a negative influence in school, can operate as a positive factor. The experimental language and reading programme appears to have counterbalanced the difficulties usually experienced in teaching 'restless' children and has made it possible for these children to transform 'disruptive restlessness' into 'constructive energy'.

This finding may seem surprising at first, but if we look more closely at the concept of 'restlessness' the finding becomes more understandable. 'Restlessness' in a classroom context has essentially two components: the energy or activity level of the child, and the degree to which this energy is educationally disruptive. If the activity level is low, it does not matter very much whether it is used disruptively or not; the child will be seen as 'quiet' and easy to teach. If the activity level of a child is high, however, it matters very much what kind of activity the child engages in. If his energy can be channelled into educationally constructive activities, the 'restless' child is likely to do better than the less energetic, the 'quiet' child. But if the energy is channelled into disruptive or destructive activities, the 'restless' child can be expected to learn very little. And so it seems reasonable that with highly active children there is more to gain if the activity is channelled the right way, but also more to lose if it is channelled the wrong way or not channelled at all.

The language and reading programme seems to have been successful in channelling the energy of 'restless' children into educationally useful activities.

It was agreed by all of us who were involved that the emphasis on various kinds of games is by far the most likely reason for this.

A follow-up evaluation using the Hunter Cloze Test

One year after the end of my original two-year evaluative study, the Inner London Education Authority's Research and Statistics Department undertook a project in order to collect some initial standardization information about the Hunter Cloze Test. It was decided that twelve of the authority's infant schools should administer the test to their top infant classes, that is, to those pupils who would be transferring to junior schools in the autumn of that year.

A representative cross-section of London infant schools was selected by the ILEA Research and Statistics Department, and the headteachers of all the selected schools agreed to participate. The headteachers were asked to estimate the proportion of their pupils who were in the lower socio-economic sector of the population. This was done in order to make it possible to establish whether the results on the Hunter Cloze Test varied with the socio-economic background of the pupils.

I decided to take the opportunity to find out how the original experimental school in my evaluative study would compare with other schools in terms of reading test results one year after the end of my study. The ILEA research team agreed to include the experimental school among the twelve schools to be tested.

It must be noted that the group of children to be tested on this occasion was an entirely new population, compared to those included in my study. They had started school one year later than my experimental pupils, and there had been no unusual 'outside' interest shown in the implementation of their curriculm, and no external monitoring of their progress by me. They had, however, been taught according to the same systematic language and reading programme as the experimental pupils one year earlier, since this was the adopted policy for the entire school.

The ILEA Research and Statistics Department distributed the Hunter Cloze Test sheets with instruction sheets, and the tests were in all cases administered by the class teacher. The completed tests were scored by members of the ILEA research team.

The test results showed a correlation between socio-economic background and test results, with the usual tendency for the mainly 'middle-class' schools to have higher mean scores than the mainly 'working-class' schools. The difference was, however, not so great that the test could be considered less suitable for the assessment of one social class than for the assessment of another.

The mean score for all schools except my original experimental school (i.e., a total of eleven schools) was 9.0, and the mean score for the original experimental school was 13.2. The difference is statistically significant, and it is sufficiently large to be of great 'practical' educational significance. In order to make the comparison as fair and hence as meaningful as possible, the original experimental school was also compared with the group of four schools which most closely resembled it in the socio-economic distribution of their pupils. The mean cloze test score for these four schools was 9.6, compared to the mean score of 13.2 for the original experimental school, that is, the difference was practically the same as when the experimental school was compared with the whole group of eleven schools in the follow-up study.

I find the significance of this result highly interesting. In the first place it supports the main conclusion of the two-year evaluative study, namely that a systematic approach to language development and reading is beneficial in terms of progress in reading ability. Secondly, it gives evidence to the effect that these benefits are not merely the result of what is often called a 'drive', or emphasis throughout the duration of the evaluative study. The results of the follow-up evaluation suggest that the systematic policy adopted by the school in question is continuing to justify the claims which are being made regarding its value.

Conclusions

The results of my evaluative study and of the ILEA follow-up study have provided evidence that the systematic language and reading programme implemented by the experimental school was of significant advantage to the great majority of pupils. On the basis of my classroom observations and of my experience of infant school work, I suggest that three major features of the experimental curriculum contributed to the marked progress of the experimental school children.

Firstly, the *system* and *structure* with which the books and materials available in this school were reorganized seem to have enhanced the efficiency of the teachers' work. In this context it was important that the staff of the experimental school cooperated closely in the development and implementation of the programme. I believe that the success achieved depended largely on the fact that the system and structure were clearly *defined*, *discussed*, *revised* where necessary, and *agreed upon* by the staff as a team. After this the schemes of work were typed and duplicated in a simple form which made it possible to have a series of record sheets for each pupil, on which his progress could be noted easily.

There was never any element of stress or pressure involved for either teacher or pupil. All the materials, apparatus, games, and reading books were of the usual attractive 'play activity' kind. But by systematically ordering them into difficulty levels, it was made possible for pupils to *play* in ways which are *educationally more valuable* with regard to language and literacy development. And pupils derived *confidence* by successfully accomplishing easier tasks before being confronted with more difficult ones. I believe that the degree of *self-confidence* which a pupil achieves during this early schooling is central to his well-being and to his future progress.

There is no doubt that the teachers involved appreciate this way of working. Some of them are young teachers, and they all agree that teachers at the beginning of their careers are very grateful to have the support of an explicitly stated and organized school policy which the whole staff accepts and implements.

The second major feature of the programme which, in my opinion, has contributed to its success, is the emphasis on *language games*. The system of language games used in the experimental school has been devised for small groups of two, three, or four children. Once taught, these games can be played with intermittent teacher supervision, thus providing a means for supplementing the language development accomplished on a one-to-one pupil-teacher relationship basis. Materials of this kind are of great value in enabling children to become more articulate and confident in their use of language, and to become more aware of the importance of choosing appropriate linguistic forms for what they want to communicate to other people.

The language games contribute to the pupils' progress in an area of education which has not been other than incidentally featured in the past, namely the development and extension of skills in spoken language. This is true of all age ranges, but it has particular importance for nursery and infant school children.

The successful use of language games within the framework of a structured programme for language and literacy has particularly interesting implications for all children – whether immigrant or native – whose environment during the preschool years has not been conducive to the development of the kind of spoken language used in schools. It is significant that 'middle-class' children, whose spoken language usually conforms well with the language used by teachers in school, normally show higher levels of attainment in reading and other aspects of literacy than 'working-class' children. This does not necessarily mean that the 'working-class' children should be helped by being taught 'middle-class' language. What many 'working-class' children need is the confidence and improved ability to express clearly, precisely, and effectively all those things they want to communicate *in the school situation*.

The experimental language and reading programme developed for this study has proved to be particularly valuable for children of 'working-class' origin. The 'working-class' children in the experimental school performed, on the average, better than the 'middle-class' children in the control school, a finding which is very unusual. It should be emphasized that the experimental programme was *not* devised as a *compensatory* programme; its major aim was to further the language and reading development of children of *all* social classes and ability levels.

The results indicate that this aim has been achieved. Compared to the control group the experimental group made accelerated progress, and so the approach benefited pupils of all abilities and of all socio-economic groups. But it is not surprising that those children who were in a position to gain most from an emphasis on language development (because their own language usage was unlike the language usage in school) made most progress.

It seems reasonable to assume that one important factor behind the unusually marked progress of 'working-class' children has been the use of language games. These games involve children in meaningful, goal-directed verbal communication, and each child is encouraged to try to express fairly complex ideas and relationships in words and to use language accurately and descriptively.

The third major feature of the successful experimental programme is one which is closely connected with the two previously mentioned, namely the more *profitable use of pupil time*. During visits to infant classes I frequently observe that, while the class teacher is hearing individual pupils reading, most of the other children are occupied with activities aimed almost exclusively at the development of creative abilities rather than cognitive abilities. I am not suggesting that creative development is not an essential part of early education. My concern is over the *balance* of activities, or more specifically about the relative absence of play activities designed to foster and extend ability in basic cognitive and communicative skills.

Teachers perhaps feel that basic skills must be taught directly, a view which is in keeping with the emphasis most teachers place on hearing their pupils read aloud as often as possible. My teaching experience and my observations in a large number of classrooms have led to the conclusion that play activities should be usefully extended to include, among all the others, group games for the development of language and prereading skills. Although the topic has not been dealt with in this book, numeracy skills can be similarly catered for in group play situations. By including in the curriculum games which promote development of cognitive and communicative skills, teachers are able to ensure that the pupils spend a larger part of their school day improving these skills.

It is arguable that too much emphasis on activities designed to develop creative skills at the expense of cognitive and communicative skills may result in education which positively discriminates in favour of 'middle-class' children. These children tend to come from more 'educationally supportive' homes, where the parents may be more likely to supplement the creative provisions of the school with provisions for cognitive and communicative development.

Given the pupil-teacher ratio in most infant schools, the pupils' time cannot be used to best advantage unless they can work *to some extent* in pairs or small groups, without constant teacher supervision. The curriculum tested in my study gives many opportunities for pupils to work in small 'self-directed' groups, where they are involved in purposeful verbal communication *with each other*. And the fact that the tasks which the children are given are carefully graded makes it possible for them to feel confident that they can cope with what they have been asked to do. The grading also helps to avoid situations where children stop playing the learning games because they are bored by tasks that are too easy and not sufficiently challenging. All this contributes to increasing the likelihood that most of the children are both happily and usefully occupied for most of the time.

It was clear from my observations of the language games in operation that benefit was being derived in the form of social training. The children were adapting to the informal classroom organization and learning to benefit from its most productive features. They were learning to listen to each other, to respond, to collaborate, and to be generally cooperative and sensitive to the needs and rights of their fellow pupils. The fostering of more independent learning strategies has not generally been regarded as an important feature of infant school education and is perhaps worthy of more serious consideration.

CHAPTER 9

THE NEED FOR CHANGE: KEY ISSUES

The 'meaningful' approach to teaching reading

> The more I thought about language and the more I read about reading research, the more convinced I became that a key mistake had been made in not *treating reading as language*, in not being concerned with how the reader gets meaning from print. (Goodman 1976, my italics)

This was how Kenneth Goodman described the first stages of his interest in the reading process, an interest which gave rise to a long-term research programme widely regarded as being one of the most important of its kind. Goodman's definition of reading is as follows:

> It is a process of getting meaning from print. And this process has two characteristics. One is that the reader is attempting to *get at meaning*. The second is that he or she is *using whole language* to do so. (op. cit., my italics)

This is the view of reading, with consequent implications for the teaching of reading, which underpins the approach to language and literacy development in the nursery and infant school advocated in this book. Although the view seems intuitively appealing and in line with common sense, it is still relatively new and the implications for teaching beginning reading are not generally accepted.

The main consequences of this lack of acceptance are the use of teaching methods and materials which do not support it. Even when Goodman's view that the reader, from the very beginning, is concerned with 'getting at meaning using whole language', the far-reaching implications of this view are not usually fully recognized. There are many teachers who agree, in principle, that reading must always be concerned with meaning, but who still continue to use materials for beginning reading which contain *very little meaning* for the young reader to 'get at'.

Another implication of this view of reading is that it engenders a need for individualized instruction, something which seems like a daunting task for the class teacher who may have to cater for a class of about thirty children. Language-based approaches to beginning reading are often criticized because of the need for a one-to-one teacher-pupil relationship during the early stages of learning. It is curious, however, that teachers and student teachers should have reservations about the approach because of the need for individualization, since most teachers are accustomed to hearing individual pupils reading throughout the years of infant schooling. There is no reason why a language-based approach should necessitate *more* time for one-to-one teacher-pupil contact than the traditional approach of hearing children read, page by page, the early books of a reading scheme (basal reading series in the U.S.A.).

It must also be pointed out that the question of how *pupil time* is spent is at least as important as the question of time for individual pupil-teacher contact in the teaching of reading. A language-based approach, utilizing language games that lead directly into reading for meaning, makes it possible to engage pupils in meaningful learning activities with only partial teacher supervision. This means that the teaching/learning process is individualized, not only for the few minutes per day the teacher can concentrate exclusively on each individual child, but for most of the time which the children spend on language and reading activities.

A language-based approach to reading is, then, not just something for the fortunate teacher who has only a small group of children to cater for. Given proper curriculum planning and selection of materials, this approach facilitates an effective organization of the teaching/learning process in any infant school classroom.

Curriculum development

If it is acknowledged that the development and extension of spoken language skills is of central importance in early education in general, and to the development of basic literacy in particular, then it must be ensured that provision for language development in the infant school is adequate. Typically, language development occurs only incidentally in the teacher-pupil interaction of the infant classroom; it is rarely given emphasis, focus, or structure. And this is likely to remain the case, unless the school staff adopts a systematized policy or curriculum for language and literacy which is given due emphasis within the wider infant school curriculum.

The task of developing a comprehensive, systematic curriculum for language and literacy development is a very difficult one, even if all members of the school's teaching staff participate in the work. Most schools will need clear and specific guidelines, if they are to succeed in this task.

The Bullock Committee did not provide any model curriculum for the infant school – or for any other school stage – since they believed that each school should endeavour to meet the special needs of its own pupils. I certainly agree that each school staff must take responsibility for tailoring the curriculum to the needs of their own pupils. But it is also my belief that there is a great deal of common ground to be covered in all infant schools, and that a 'sample' core curriculum which is based on a carefully structured series of educational objectives would be very valuable as a guide to the development of the individual school curriculum. It must be emphasized that the existence of a 'sample' curriculum in no way implies that this curriculum should be centrally imposed or prescribed. The aim would only be to provide a 'model' or 'models' for individual schools to use as a starting point.

It is important that any guidelines or 'sample' curriculum in this area are developed through a cooperative effort where experience from individual schools is utilized. It is, in this context, very pleasing to be able to record the fact that in my many requests for cooperation, involving countless infant school headteachers and teachers, I have encountered universal interest and enthusiasm. This is true not only of London teachers, but of those in a great many parts of England, Scotland, and Wales, who have been involved in the standardization of the Hunter-Grundin Literacy Profiles. In my opinion, this response gives evidence of a high degree of professionalism, and of a very active interest in curriculum development, both of which bode well for the prospects of future cooperative ventures in this field.

In one of the 'keynote' lectures at the 1977 UKRA Conference, Michael Marland emphasized the need for a 'professional synthesis' in the field of reading generally (see Hunter-Grundin and Grundin, 1978). Such a synthesis is certainly needed in the field of the infant school language and literacy curriculum.

This professional synthesis can only be brought about by the combined efforts of local education authorities, teacher training establishments, libraries, publishing firms, and heads and teachers with experience of the multi-faceted problems involved.

Development of teaching/learning materials

A 'model' curriculum for language and reading development in the infant school, useful as I believe it to be, is likely to seem utopian to most teachers, unless materials are available which correspond to and support the curriculum in practical classroom terms. This would entail the development of classroom materials by means of which young pupils can achieve the series of educational objectives specified in the 'model' core curriculum. Such materials should primarily be in the form of language and reading games, which can be played by small groups of children with, after having been taught, intermittent teacher supervision. The games should progress towards the incorporation of reading materials of various kinds, thus gradually involving the pupils in reading as a purposeful and pleasurable activity which uses language and vocabulary familiar to the pupils.

From the beginning, the series of materials should aim at the parallel development of listening, speaking, reading, and writing as interrelated and interdependent skills. Individual record sheets should form an integrated part of these allied materials, and should be designed in such a way that they facilitate the monitoring of individual pupil progress. Items in each set of materials should be graded, so that children can always be given tasks of an appropriate difficulty level – the appropriateness being determined by monitoring of individual progress, and by the professional judgement of the teacher.

The materials will need to provide a great variety, both in terms of content and in terms of difficulty levels, but all materials will need to have one thing in common: that they involve children in communication through *meaningful language*, whether it be oral or written language.

Teacher education

It goes without saying that improvements in teacher education, both at initial and at inservice levels, are central to the introduction and implementation of successful language and reading policies in infant schools. This necessitates the provision of improved courses focusing on the practical implications of our present knowledge about language and reading development in young children. Teachers need to have both the theoretical insight into various methods of evaluation and assessment and the practical skills that enable them to apply these methods in their classroom work. Evaluation of pupils' skills is necessary for the proper monitoring of progress, but evaluation of materials and of teaching methods or 'strategies' is equally important.

Ideally, all teachers should be equipped to take responsibility for implementing a systematic, structured language and reading policy for the children in their clases. This would, however, call for a massive programme of both initial and inservice training, which, for economic reasons, is unlikely to be achieved within the foreseeable future. Even the relatively modest goal of providing every school with a language and reading specialist can only be reached through a large-scale, national 'inservice' training campaign. Local education authorities must order their financial priorities so that funds are available to cover the cost of inservice courses and to permit at least part-time release from normal teaching duties for the teachers who take these courses. Institutions of higher education should as a matter of priority, offer incentives such as study leave to members of their staff to specialize in areas related to language and literacy. At the same time it is extremely important that academic teaching related to the language and reading development of young children remains closely rooted to classroom practice. Ideally, teacher training should be organized so that knowledge derived from the more theoretical studies can be directly implemented and evaluated in the course of classroom work.

Language across the curriculum

The fourth of the Bullock Report's seventeen principal recommendations is that

> Each school should have an organized policy for *language across the curriculum*, establishing every teacher's involvement in language and reading develop-

ment throughout the years of schooling. (my italics)

It is true that this relates more to the later stages of primary education, and more specifically to secondary schools, where language and reading development are rarely given much emphasis, except for those pupils who are considered to be in need of remedial reading instruction. The report recommends reappraisal of the curriculum in all subject areas in order to include provision for the development and extension of spoken language ability and of reading skills – including average and above average skills. Pupils should be taught to use more effectively the books required for study within each subject area. And equally other communication skills in relation to each subject area should be extended.

There are however, implications of the *infant school* language curriculum discussed in this book which relate to the recommendation quoted above. The language games described help to develop in pupils not only greater confidence and facility in spoken language usage, but also valuable attitudes to, and techniques of, enquiry which enhance the pupil's personal involvement in learning situations of all kinds. In other words the techniques involved in playing group language games can be profitably extended within the infant school to include learning in the fields of mathematics, science, etc. What is required is the organization of learning materials for suitable topics in such a way that a small group of children can collaborate in sharing a learning experience during which they will have more personal involvement, responsibility, and control of the situation. This would provide, for an *organized language-based 'discovery' approach* to some of the teaching/learning in the infant school. Observation of the degree to which young children normally maintain active interest in the language games has led me to believe that there are important implications for curriculum development along these lines, and for wider evaluative studies.

False dichotomies

There is a tendency among teachers to adopt a particular method to the exclusion of *any part* of other methods. John Dewey warned educationists of this in the early years of this century. He called this manner of polarizing issues regarding teaching methods 'dualism' – a way of perceiving different teaching practices as being either wholly right or wholly wrong, all good or all bad, and therefore each one only to be used *totally* or not at all.

This 'dualism', I find, is particularly in evidence in the field of early education, and it results it some false dichotomies which are worthy of discussion.

For example, it is often argued that young children derive so much benefit from play that the introduction of any kind of 'system' would be unnatural and undesirable. It must be pointed out, though, that it is the *teacher* who is expected to be 'systematic' in her approach, in order that pupils will benefit from all the valuable experiences the infant school has to offer. It is the teacher's systematic planning and implementation of the curriculum which will enable the children to gain the confidence which is achieved by encountering learning tasks in a gradually increasing order of difficulty.

It has been argued that the most valuable way of developing language skills in young children is through the teacher's exploitation of real, meaningful situations which arise in everyday classroom work. There is no doubt about the value of this approach to language development. But this does not mean that teachers should not also employ other methods of fostering and extending language skills. The situations which arise spontaneously must be utilized as much as possible as means of stimulating language development. But they may not be enough, and therefore further provision for language development must be planned systematically.

The system of language games which was included in the infant school curriculum and evaluated in my study was an *addition* to the provision of games and activities in the school. The valuable teacher-pupil dialogue during meaningful activities continued to be an important part of the children's education, and was not abandoned at any time.

The main argument for the systematic use of language games stems from the concern that an important basic skill like language cannot be left *entirely* to chance encounters and incidental dialogue in the classroom. Valuable as they are, these opportunities need to be complemented by 'planned intervention' as the Bullock Report advises.

With regard to reading progress, it may be argued that the best way of improving children's reading ability is by helping them to read books, and by providing books which are as appealing as possible. This is certainly an important aim, but it must be emphasized that a systematic use of language games does not imply a neglect of books.

In giving children more opportunities to extend their language skills, it is

T _6 **

hoped that the language contained in books will be more accessible to them. There is no question of playing language games at the expense of reading books. The two kinds of experience should be interrelated and interdependent, and books should remain in their normal, vital place in the child's school life.

It is only by avoiding the trap of false dichotomies that we can make sound decisions about the full range of educational experiences which young pupils should enjoy.

Teaching 'styles'

Finally, it is worth emphasizing that my experience and research results show clearly the facile nature of dichotomies like formal-informal, traditional-progressive, and didactic-exploratory. The successfully implemented language and reading curriculum in the infant school makes it possible for children to work in a situation which combines the positive features of supposedly irreconcilable approaches to teaching. This situation can be described as 'structured informality', or as 'didactically organized exploration'. The curriculum preserves all that is excellent in the British infant school tradition, in that it is based on children's play, but is at the same time truly progressive in that it gives a special role to play, a role determined by a modern view of education as a systematic goal-directed activity. Through this curriculum children are enabled to make a very successful start towards literacy.

APPENDICES

Appendix 1 Contains the school booklet which the experimental school (Bessemer Grange) gives to all parents several weeks before their child enters the school. Close links are maintained with parents throughout the time the child attends the school and the booklet is revised regularly, as changes are made and new ventures undertaken. A joint committee of teachers and parents are currently producing a book which will describe a variety of out-of-school visits and home activities which would support and implement the work of the school. Through these efforts, the parents are made aware of the aims of the school concerning their children's education and are enabled to subscribe to these aims.

Appendix 2 Contains a selection of the experimental curriculum 'ladders', which were reproduced to become individual pupil record sheets. These relate to the materials used in the school, and are regularly revised as new materials are included.

Appendix 3 Contains the tables relating to the evaluation of the experimental curriculum through action research.

APPENDIX 1

Bessemer Grange Infants' School
Booklet for Parents

We welcome you to Bessemer Grange Infants' School and hope this leaflet will be helpful to you. Over the school year it will be supplemented with letters giving specific details of meetings, holidays and school events. If you find something vital has been left out, do let us know.

We hope you and your child will have a happy and successful time at our school.

Aims and Organisation.

General Aim of the School.

Our aim is to foster the development of a literate, numerate person able to take advantage of all aspects of his own and outside resources whether they be intellectual or physical. We set the development within the social framework of a happy, thriving school.

We organise to achieve this in the following ways:

Curriculum

We are a school staff agreeing with the Plowden Committee 'that play is vital to a child's learning' but are firmly committed to the structural development of such learning. *Our priorities are literacy and numeracy*, while at the same time being deeply aware of the value of *creative activities, music, drama, science* and *physical education*.

We have a school *language programme* which includes a set reading scheme and there is a daily concentrated reading time throughout the school when three teachers may be present doing reading with one class. There is a school mathematics syllabus and number work, like reading, is done in flexible ability groups.

Creative work includes painting, printing, collage, claywork, plasterwork, woodwork, dyeing, cooking, weaving, sewing, wendyhouse play, big brick play, sand and water play, construction toys (Meccano etc.) and model making.

Science activities including nature study, also cover simple electric circuits, magnetism, light, mirrors, reflection and sand and water experiments. Many topics may evolve, and be extended beyond the classroom situation, by visits and excursions.

Musically we aim through singing, instrument playing and musical movement to create an awareness and recognition of rhythm and time. The older children have the opportunity to play the recorder, which is at present taught by mothers. Volunteers needed!

In *drama* we encourage self-expression through mime, movement and acting. At Christmas the whole school is involved in an entertainment presented to Parents.

In *physical education* we encourage the development of the basic skills as well as extending the mental stimulation that can come from physical activity. We have large gymnastic apparatus such as a climbing frame, benches and stools, as well as small apparatus such as bats, balls and skipping ropes.

None of these subjects are taught in isolation. They are integrated so that, for example, a group making buns in cooking would also be doing number work in weighing and counting as well as being expected to record what they did afterwards. Project work particularly would include all these areas being worked together. In a recent Red Indian project not only did the class research and write about Red Indians but also maths work was done, e.g. measuring the totem pole they had made; Red Indian songs were learnt; Red Indian dances created; teepees, clothes, canoes made; and experiments carried out in print-making.

Preparation for School.

Parents whose children are about to start school often ask – 'What can I do to help my child?'

Here are some suggestions –

i.   Talk to your child. Encourage him/her to ask questions. Try to find time to answer his/her questions.

ii.   Read stories to your child. Discuss the story afterwards.

iii. Take your child to the local library to choose a story book.

iv.   Sing nursery rhymes together.

v.   Watch television with your child. Talk about the programme.

vi.   Encourage your child to notice the world around him/her and remark on what he sees. e.g. If you are taking him shopping, encourage him to notice anything different, e.g. men repairing telephones, 'What are they doing?' etc.

vii. Count things together. e.g. knives and forks, the stairs as you walk up them.

If your child *wants* to practise writing his/her name, show him, using the following letter shapes –

Aa Bb Cc Dd Ee Ff Gg Hh Ii Jj Kk Ll Mm Nn
Oo Pp Qq Rr Ss Tt Uu Vv Ww Xx Yy Zz

e.g. John Smith. (*only* use capitals for the *initial* letters).

Encourage your child to dress himself/herself (gradually mastering one item of clothing at a time!)

Show your child how to blow his/her nose.

Teach your child how to use the toilet without help.

Teach your child how to use a knife and fork.

Encourage your child to learn his/her address.

Children.

The children are organised into 7 infant classes and 2 part-time nursery classes (a.m and p.m.) The top 5 classes are organised according to age; the 2 lower classes are verticallya grouped within the age range of one year. There are times when the whole school is together in an assembly, and teaching can be organised in a class, group or individual situation. Groups can be either organised according to ability or be of mixed ability, depending upon the activity involved.

Staff.

At present there are 10 full-time members of the teaching staff including the Head and the Deputy Head. In addition the school has three part-time teachers. There are 9 ancillary helpers who include 'dinner ladies' and a secretary. We share a caretaker and his assistant with the Junior school.

Four members of our teaching staff have extra responsibility posts in language, creative activities, science/audio visual aids and the library. The Deputy Head at present covers mathematics. These post holders encourage the development of their subject area throughout the school.

Parents.

We have an active P.T.A. which new parents are particularly encouraged to join. An Annual General Meeting for all parents is held in September at which a committee of parents and teachers is elected.

A governor is also on the committee. The committee aims to represent the parents' views and also raise funds for school equipment and arrange social functions and outings. Various workshops, (which demonstrate the school's teaching methods in a practical way), discussions and talks are organised, as well as social and fund raising events.

If parents wish to raise particular matters at P.T.A. meetings would they please contact any P.T.A. member as listed in the 'Who's Who' (end of this booklet).

The school is open to parents every Tuesday morning to enable them to visit their child's classroom to see their own child's work as well as being able to look round the whole school if they wish.

Parents' help in the classroom is welcomed. We are very anxious to make use of all your talents. In the past parents have taken groups for cookery, language work, woodwork, chess, recorder practice, etc. Class teachers are happy to exploit you in any way!

An evening meeting is arranged for parents to meet and discuss their child's progress with his/her class teacher. During the summer term a meeting is arranged to enable parents to see their child's primary school record.

The Head is readily available. The most convenient time is at 9.10 a.m. or 3.00 p.m. but other appointment times can be easily made.

Governors.

We have a Board of Governors jointly with the Junior School. The Governors meet every term and their job is 'in consultation with the Head teacher to exercise *oversight* of the conduct and curriculum of the school.' The parents of the Infants' School elect two parents every 4 years to become parent governors on this board. The election meeting is advertised well in advance.

General Information

There are other areas of our organisation you will need to know about –

1. School times.   2. School dinners.   3. Play Centre.
4. Library.   5. Fire drill.   6. Outings.
7. Medicals.   8. Accidents.

1. *School times.*
   Infants'   9.10 – 12.00 noon.
                     1.20 – 3.30 p.m.
   Nursery   9.15 – 11.45 a.m.
                     1.00 – 3.30 p.m.

The Library.

As well as a recently re-organised resource area (which includes our non-fiction books as well as picture tapes etc.) we have a library area near Class 2 and also class book corners. We now have a lending library for children in their last year with us. Books are changed every Friday. We hope to extend this facility to more children as we acquire more books. The P.T.A. runs a library for parents every Tuesday afternoon. This has a selection of education books and story books to read to children.

Fire Drill.

The whole school has a fire drill practice every term.

Outings.

We have a great variety of outings throughout the year, sometimes on a class basis, sometimes involving more of the school. There are ILEA rules as to supervision and parents are given details of any such outings and their consent is required.

Play Centre.

A play centre operates in the school hall after school until 6.00 p.m. It is organised separately from the school but children bringing money to spend there can have it looked after by the class teacher. There is a money limit of 7p. There is *no* Play Centre on Friday afternoons.

APPENDIX 2

Sample units of work schemes in the experimental language and reading programme

Prereading

Game	Introduced	Practised	Learned
12 Match 4-letter group			
11 Match 3-letter group			
10 Match 2-letter group			
9 Match single letter			
8 More difficult Snap			
7 Simple Snap			
6 Match Parts to Pictures			
5 Pictures (fine detail)			
4 Pictures			
3 Shape: Pictures			
2 Patterns of Shapes			
1 Basic Shapes			

Learning Materials Service (ILEA)
Language Development
Instruction Tapes

Name: ....Teacher: ....

Book	Description of taped 'game'	Date completed
8	Prepositions	
7	Monster Anatomy	
6	Sound Book	
5	Puzzles and picture making	
4	Puzzles	
3	Illustrating a story	
2	Picture making: Stage 2	
1	Picture making: Stage 1	

The evaluation of the experimental curriculum through action research

Table 1 Number of children pretested (at age five) and finally tested (at age seven) in the experimental school and in the seven different control schools.

School	No. pretested age 5	No. not pretested age 5	Total no. tested age 7
Experimental	15*	49	64
Control 1	25	48	73
2	27	86	113
3	36	33	69
4	29	–	29
Control 5	–	85	85
6	–	20	20
7	–	73	73
Sum	132	394	526

* Total number of children in the class was 24, but 9 children had nursery school experience and were therefore excluded from the data analysis.

Table 2   Summary of certain background data for the five schools in which pretestings were carried out.

Variable	Experi-mental school	Control school				All control schools
		1	2	3	4	
Age in months	60.4	60.6	60.3	61.7	61.1	61.1
Percent boys	47	48	41	53	41	46
Percent girls	53	52	59	47	59	54
Percent lower working class	27	16	63	50	34	42
Percent upper working class	40	56	33	42	38	42
Percent non-working class	33	28	4	8	28	18
Reading readiness score	22.6	22.4	12.9	16.6	24.4	18.9
General ability score	40.8	44.4	38.7	41.7	47.6	43.1

Table 3   Test results for the pretested and monitored groups at the end of the two-year evaluation period (at age seven): Experimental group, E, and control groups, C1 – C4. (Total no. of children = 132, nos. for each subgroup are given in Table 1.)

Variable		E	C1	C2	C3	C4	All C groups	Diff. E-All C
Hunter	M	14.2	2.0	3.0	2.9	8.4	4.1	Sign.
Cloze Test	s	5.5	2.7	3.9	4.4	8.6	6.0	
Attitude to	M	2.7	2.5	2.4	2.4	2.7	2.5	N.S.
Reading	s	0.5	0.7	0.6	0.7	0.5	0.7	
Attitude to	M	2.9	2.3	2.6	2.6	2.8	2.6	N.S.
Cloze Test	s	0.4	0.7	0.6	0.6	0.4	0.6	

M = mean value
s = standard deviation
Sign.   means that difference between experimental (E) and total control group (All C) is statistically significant.
N.S.   means that this difference is not statistically significant.

Table 4   Background and posttest data for the experimental (E) and control groups (C1 – C7) in the larger, unmonitored sample of children (Total no. = 394; nos. for different subgroups are given in Table 1.)

Variable	E	C1	C2	C3	C5	C6	C7	All C groups	Diff. E–All C
Percent boys	55	60	52	70	45	49	56	55	N.S.
Percent girls	45	40	48	30	55	51	44	45	N.S.
Percent lower working class	25	19	17	39	20	44	7	24	N.S.
Percent upper working class	51	63	42	27	35	38	38	41	N.S.
Percent non-working class	24	19	41	33	45	18	55	35	N.S.
Percent restless pupils	31	29	21	24	5	25	25	23	N.S.
Attitude to reading (percent 'like')	76	69	54	76	85	60	47	60	Sign.
Attitude to cloze test (percent 'like')	74	42	79	61	60	69	78	68	N.S.
Hunter Cloze Test score	17.6	4.1	13.8	9.2	9.5	5.6	7.8	8.5	Sign.

N.S. = not statistically significant difference between experimental (E) and all control groups (All C).
Sign. = significant difference between E and All C.
Note   that the numbering of the control groups is the same as in Table 1, which means that school no. 4 is not included because it had no pupils in this (unmonitored) category.

BIBLIOGRAPHY

Adams, O. (1936) 'Implications of language in beginning reading', *Childhood Education*, pp. 158–162.

Barnes, D. (1971) 'Classroom contexts for language and learning', *Educational Review*, vol. 23, pp. 235-247.

Bellugi-Klima, U. (1970) *The Acquisition of Negation in Children's Speech*, Cambridge, Mass.: MIT Press.

Bereiter, C. and Engelmann, S. (1966) *Teaching Disadvantaged Children in the Pre-School*, New Jersey: Prentice-Hall.

Bernstein, B. (1972) 'Education Cannot Compensate for Society'. In: A. Cashdan and E. Grugeon (eds.), *Language in Education*, London: The Oxford University Press/Routledge & Kegan Paul.

Blank, M. Rose, S.A. and Berlin, L.J. (1978) *The Language of Learning: The Pre-School Years*, New York: Grune & Stratton.

Bormuth, J.R. (1967) 'Comparable cloze and multiple-choice comprehension test scores', *Journal of Reading*, vol. 10, pp. 291-299.

Bormuth, J.R. (1969) 'Factor validity of cloze tests as measures of reading comprehension ability', *Reading Research Quarterly*, vol. 4, pp. 358-365.

Briggs, L.J. (1968) *Handbook of Procedures for the Design of Instruction*,

Pittsburgh: AIR.

Brown, R. (1973) *A First Language in the Early Stages*, London: Allen and Unwin.

Buros, I.K. (1959) *The Fifth Mental Measurement Yearbook*, Highland Park, N.J.: Gryphon Press.

Carrillo, L.W. (1978) 'Equal Opportunity in reading'. In: E. Hunter-Grundin and H.U. Grundin (eds.) *Reading: Implementing the Bullock Report*, London: UKRA/Ward Lock Educational.

Cashdan, A. and Grugeon, E. (eds.) (1972) *Language in Education: A Source Book*, London: The Oxford University Press/Routledge & Kegan Paul.

Cazden, C.B. (1969) 'Suggestions from studies of early language acquisition', *Childhood Education*, pp. 127-131.

Chomsky, C. (1972) 'Stages in language development and reading exposure', *Harvard Educational Review*, vol. 42, pp. 1-33.

Chomsky, N. (1957) *Syntactic Structures*, The Hague: Mouton.

Chomsky, N. (1965) *Aspects of the Theory of Syntax*, Cambridge, Mass: M.I.T. Press.

Davies, I.K. and Hartley, J. (1972) *Contributions to an Educational Technology*, London: Butterworth.

Davidson, H.P. (1931) *Genetic Psychology, No. 9.*, 1931.

Day, D.E. (1974) 'Language instruction for young children: What ten years of confusion has taught us', *Interchange*, vol. 5, pp. 59-72.

Dearden, R.F. (1972) ' "Needs" in education'. In: R.F. Dearden, P.H. Hirst and R.S. Peters (eds.), *Education and the Development of Reason*, London: Routledge & Kegan Paul.

Dechant, E.V. and Smith, H.P. (1977) *Psychology in Teaching Reading*, 2nd edition, New Jersey: Prentice-Hall.

D.E.S. (Department of Education and Science) (1975) *A Language for Life*. Report of the Committee of Inquiry appointed by the Secretary of State for Education and Science under the Chairmanship of Sir Alan Bullock, London: HMSO.

D.E.S. (1959) *Primary Education*, HMSO.

D.E.S. (1978) *Primary Education in England*, HMSO.

D.E.S. (1978) *Progress in Education*, HMSO.

Dunkin, M.J. and Biddle, B.J. (1974) *The Study of Teaching*, New York: Holt, Rinehart & Winston.

Durkin, D. (1970) 'What Does Research Say about the Time to Begin Reading ?' *Journal of Educational Research*, 64 (October 1970), pp. 51-56.

Emans, R. and Fox, S.E. (1973) 'Teaching behaviours in reading instruction', *The Reading Teacher*, vol. 23, pp. 142-148.

Fleming, J.T. (1968) 'Oral language and beginning reading: Another look', *The Reading Teacher*, vol. 22, pp. 24-29.

Flesch, R. (1955) *Why Johnny Can't Read*, New York: Harpers.

Gage, N.L. (1972) *Teacher Effectiveness and Teacher Education*, Palo Alto: Pacific.

Gagné, R.M. (1965) *The Conditions of Learning*, New York: Holt, Rinehart & Winston.

Gahagan, D.M. and Gahagan, G.A. (1970) *Talk Reform — Explorations in Language for Infant School Children*, London: Routledge & Kegan Paul.

Gates, A.I. (1937) 'The Necessary Mental Age for Beginning Reading', *Elementary School Journal* (March 1937), pp. 497-508.

Gill, V.M. (1971) 'Factors affecting the reading skills of 6½ – 7 year old children. Unpublished M.Lit. thesis, Edinburgh University.

Goldberg, M.L. (1967) 'Adapting teacher style to pupil differences: teachers for disadvantaged children'. In: A.H. Passow, M. Goldberg and A.J. Tennenbaum, *Education of the Disadvantaged*, New York: Holt, Rinehart & Winston, pp. 465-482.

Goodacre, E. (1967) *Reading in Infant Classes*, Slough: N.F.E.R.

Goodman, K. (1970) 'Reading: a psycholinguistic guessing game'. In: H. Singer and R.B. Ruddell (eds.) *Theoretical Models and Processes of Reading*, Newark: IRA, pp. 259-272.

Goodman, K. (1976) *Reading: a Conversation with Kenneth Goodman*, New York: Scott, Foresman & Co.

Goodman, K., (ed.) (1977) *Miscues Analysis: Application to Reading Instruction*, Urbana, Illinois: NCTE.

Goodman, K.S., Goodman, Y.M., and Burke, C. (1978) 'Reading for life: the psycholoinguistic base', In: E. Hunter-Grundin and H.U. Grundin (eds.), *Reading: Implementing the Bullock Report*, London: UKRA/Ward Lock Educational.

Gross, N., Giacquinta, J.B. and Bernstein, M. (1971) *Implementing Organizational Innovations*, An Open University Set Book, New York: Harper & Row.

Grundin, H.U., *et al.* (1978) 'Cloze Procedure and Comprehension: An Exploratory Study Across Three Languages', In: D. Feitelson (ed.), *Cross-Cultural Perspectives on Reading and Reading Research*, Newark: IRA.

Halliday, M.A.K. (1973) *Explorations in the Function of Grammar*, London: Edward Arnold.

Halliday, M.A.K. (1969) 'Relevant models of language', In: *Educational Review*, vol. 22, pp. 26-27.

Heilman, A.W. (1972) *Principles and Practices of Teaching Reading*, 3rd edition, Columbus, Ohio: Merrill.

Hildreth, G. (1958) *Teaching Reading*, New York: Holt, Rinehart & Winston.

Holt, J. (1964) *How Children Fail*, London: Pitman.

Hunter, E. (1977) *Reading Skills: A Systematic Approach*, Guidelines 3, London: Council for Educational Technology.

Hunter-Grundin, E. and Grundin, H.U. (eds.) (1978) *Reading: Implementing the Bullock Report*, London: UKRA/Ward Lock Educational.

Hunter-Grundin, E. and Grundin, H.U. (1979) *The Hunter-Grundin Literacy Profiles. Level ONE*, The Test Agency, Cournswood House, North Dean, High Wycombe, Bucks.

Jenkinson, M.D. (1957) 'Selected Processes and Difficulties in Reading Comprehension', Unpublished, doctoral dissertation, University of Chicago.

Kusmina, N.V. (1963) 'The process of forming pedagogical abilities: a Soviet contribution', In: *Yearbook of Education*, 1963, Evans Bros. in association with the University of London Institute of Education and Columbia University, pp. 95-102.

Lawton, D. (1968) *Social Class, Language and Education*, London: Routledge & Kegan Paul.

Loban, W.D. (1968) *Social Class, Language and Education* London: Routledge & Kegan Paul.

Loban W.D. (1968) *The Language of Elementary School Children*, Research Report No. 1., National Council of Teachers of English, Champaign, Illinois.

Manning, K. and Sharp, A. (1977) *Structuring Play in the Early Years*, London: Ward Lock/Drakes.

McCarthy, D. (1954) 'Language development in children', In: L. Carmichael (ed.), *Manual of Child Psychology*, 2nd edition, New York: McGraw-Hill.

Macdonald-Ross, M. (1975) 'Behavioural objectives: a critical review', In: M. Golby, J. Greenwalk and R. West (eds.), *Curriculum Design*, An Open University Set Book, London: Croom Helm, pp. 366-386.

Medley, D.M. (1972) 'Early history of research on teacher behaviour', *International Review of Education*, vol. 18, pp. 430-439.

Melnik, A. and Merritt, J. (1972) *The Reading Curriculum*, London: University of London Press/The Oxford Unversity Press.

Morphett, M.V. and Washburne, C. (1931) 'When should children begin to read?', *Elementary School Journal*, vol. 31, pp. 496-503.

Moyle, D. (1970) *The Teaching of Reading*, London: Ward Lock Educational.

MacGinitie W.H. (1969) 'Evaluating Readiness for Learning to Read , A Critical Review and Evaluation of Research,' *Reading Research Quarterly* (Spring 1969), pp. 396-410.

Pearce, J. (1975) 'Some recent research in spoken language acquisition', *Spoken English*, vol. 8, pp. 107-110.

Peters, M. (1971) *Friends in Reading Schemes*, Cambridge: Cambridge Institute of Education.

Popham, W.J. and Baker, E.L. (1970) *Systematic Instruction*, Englewood Cliffs: Prentice-Hall.

Pumfrey, D. (1976) *Reading: Tests and Assessment Techniques*, A UKRA Teaching of Reading Monograph, London: Hodder & Stoughton.

Rankin, E.F., Jr. (1962) 'The definition of reading comprehension', *First Yearbook of the North Central Reading Association*, pp. 15-31.

Ransom, P.E. (1968) 'Determining reading levels of elementary school children by cloze testing', In: J.A. Figurel (ed.), *Forging Ahead in Reading*, IRA Convention Proceedings, vol. 12, part 1, Newark, Del.: IRA, pp. 477-482.

Reid, J.F. (1966) 'Learning to think about reading', *Educational Research*, vol. 9, pp. 56-62.

Reynell, J. and Huntley, R.M.C. (1971) 'New scales for the assessment of language development in young children', *Journal of Learning Disabilities*. vol. 4, pp. 549-557.

Rowntree, D. (1974) *Educational Technology in Curriculum Development*, London: Harper & Row.

Rowntree, D. (1977) *Assessing Students: How shall we know them?* London: Harper & Row.

Simons, D. (1971) 'Reading comprehension: The need for a new perspective', *Reading Research Quarterly*, vol. 6, pp. 338-363.

Skinner, B.F. (1957) *Verbal Behaviour*, New York: Appleton-Century-Crofts.

Slobin, D.I. (1968) 'Imitation and grammatical development in children', In: N.S. Endler, L.R. Boulter and H. Osser (eds.), *Contemporary Issues in Developmental Psychology*, New York: Holt, Rinehart & Winston.

Smith, F. (1971) *Understanding Reading: A Psycholinguistic Analysis of Reading and Learning to Read*, New York: Holt, Rinehart & Winston.

Smith, F. (1973) *Psycholinguistics and Reading*, New York: Holt, Rinehart & Winston.

Smith, F. (1978) *Reading*, Cambridge: Cambridge University Press.

Standish, E.J. (1960) 'Group tests of reading readiness', *Educational Research*, vol. 2, pp. 155-160.

Taylor, P.H. (1970) '*How Teachers Plan Their Courses: Studies in Curriculum Planning*', Slough: NFER.

Templin, M.C. (1957) *Certain Language Skills in Children*, University of Minnesota Press.

Downing, J. and Thackray, D. (1975) *Reading Readiness*, 2nd edition, London: Hodder & Stoughton.

Tough, J. (1974) *Focus on Meaning*, London: Allen & Unwin.

Tough, J. (1976) *The Development of Meaning: A Study of Children's Use of Language*, London: Allen & Unwin.

Vygotsky, L.S. (1962) *Thought and Language*, Cambridge, Mass: M.I.T. Press.

Weintraub, S. (1968) 'Research: oral language and reading', *The Reading Teacher*, vol. 21, pp. 769-773.

Weir, R.H. (1962) *Language in the Crib*, The Hague: Mouton.

Wheeler, D.K. (1967) *Curriculum Process*, London: University of London Press.

Wight, J. 'Speech acts: thought acts,' *Educational Review* 28(3), pp. 168-179.

INDEX